What the Heck Is Leadership and Why Should I Care?

Endorsements

"In a sea of leadership book after leadership book, this is the one I want you to read. Why may you ask? Ultimately, it's because Gary DePaul is a great leader, a talented academic mind, a great teacher, an inspirational storyteller, and a cat person. In *What the Heck*, Gary exceptionally brings together his work experience, his studies, and his teaching acumen to truly guide his reader to think through core leadership insights, reflect, and improve. Add to that Gary's lighthearted and humorous style and you have this book. Read it now."

John S. Minutaglio
Chief Technology Officer
Strategic Link Consulting

"I have been saying for years that leadership is both an art and a science, and you have to understand the science before you can paint the portrait of organizational success. Gary's interpretation of this leadership science is thought-provoking, inspiring, and really a joy to read. While reading these pages, try to imagine how Gary's leadership approach fits with your leadership style, and in turn, engaging your workforce."

Chris Cebollero
Best Selling Author
Motivational Speaker

"*What the Heck Is Leadership and Why Should I Care?* builds on new perspectives in our ever-changing workforce. This is the decade to become relevant and purposeful as we support new leaders, create mentorships, and become change agents to become the leader our society and organizations are seeking now.

Gary's stories are relevant to what is needed to build a successful journey in leadership today. There is no better time than the present to change, learn, and expand your leadership competencies. His last Book, *Nine Practices of 21st Century Leadership*, is a must-read and his current book provides insight and advice from first-line managers to management to Senior Leaders to the CEO.

There are great leaders whose presence are known, and we are following them now, but we need to re-skill and re-tool those leaders for tomorrow's challenges and transformation."

Janet Foster
VP Senior Career Consultant
Lee Hecht Harrison

"In his new book, *What the Heck Is Leadership and Why Should I Care?*, Dr. Gary DePaul has done it again! With a bit of humor and candor, Dr. DePaul shares seven leadership principles that can lead both you and your business to remarkable success. Most importantly, the compelling stories, practices, and principles can help the experienced leader, emerging leader, and aspiring leader. This book is a must-read for anyone leading people."

Lisa J. Wicker, Ph.D.
President & CEO, Linwick & Associates, LLC
Publisher, Career Mastered Magazine

"The constituents of the CEO and top corporate executives of all companies have always been very clear and typically include shareholders, employees, and the communities they serve. However, many executive teams have under-invested in their communities, not fully understanding or embracing their potential impact. Today, it is more important for corporate executives to be effective civic leaders. The role of leadership continually rebalances investment required among constituents; thus, the approaches to lead successfully also evolve.

What the Heck explains the foundation of today's leadership in simple terms that all executives and corporate leaders, and aspiring leaders, can understand. Gary embraces and enlightens us with a pragmatic approach that challenges traditional thinking and reties business leadership to social responsibility. No longer can contemporary organizations ignore societal challenges. If executives did what Gary describes, they could begin addressing the societal problems that complicate their goals and business objectives. Gary's contemporary leadership approaches are a must-read for today's C-Suite executives!"

Michael Jones
Vice Chairman
Ranpak Holdings

"It is a pleasure to recommend Dr. Gary DePaul's new book, *What the Heck is Leadership and Why should I Care?* Gary's informal writing style and ability to utilize storytelling and humor, make for an easy read and offers useful tips for anyone seeking to learn grow and develop as a Leader."

Michael J. LaVallee
Managing Partner
Jobplex, Inc., a DHR International Company

"If you have worked for a great leader, horrible leader, or have the desire to be better at leadership, then this book is a fantastic tool. This is not an academic book about leadership, filled with lengthy theories and pages of how the study was completed to support various principles. Gary introduces concepts with personal, compelling stories. He then clarifies and succinctly provides a digestible explanation. If you are someone that has studied leadership, you'll discover that this book challenges traditional leadership assumptions. The book is a great investment of time for all leaders and aspiring leaders."

Phyllis M. Millikan
Executive Vice President
Client Solutions & Partnerships

"Gary DePaul has written a must-read book for those who call themselves a manager or a leader—or who wants to be one. In *What the Heck is Leadership and Why Should I Care?*, DePaul explains the big difference between management and leadership. And, through easy-to-read "that sounds familiar" stories, he shares his seven principles of leadership that you'll be motivated to incorporate right away."

Andrea L. Overman
Partner & Chief Marketing Officer
Chief Outsiders

"While I don't quite share Gary's passion for cats, I certainly share his passion for leadership! Through a whimsical writing style, memorable stories and the latest research and insights, Gary brings to life the *otherness* of leadership—believing, connecting and collaborating with others, putting others first, giving others control and power, and encouraging others to change and develop. Business leaders would do well to read and apply any number of the many nuggets found in this gem of a book."

Andy Fiol
Executive Vice President
Consumer & Small Business Banking, Fulton Bank
Former Executive at Capital One and Bank of America

What the Heck Is Leadership and Why Should I Care?

Gary A. DePaul, PhD

Foreword by Dave Sanderson

Independently Published
Charlotte, NC

Copyright © 2020 Gary A. DePaul, PhD

Third Printing, 07 September 2020

Thank you for purchasing the authorized edition of *What the Heck Is Leadership and Why Should I Care?* Please acquire written permission from Gary A. DePaul, PhD to reproduce or transmit any part of this book.

The author has published this book to impart authoritative knowledge about leadership from a business context. However, the scope of this book is not intended to serve as legal, professional, or consultative advice. The author cannot assume responsibility for how the consequences of the use of the book's contents.

For bulk purchases at a discounted rate, contact the author through the website, https://www.garyadepaul.com/Contact.

ISBN-13: 979-8657524260
ASIN: B08DT1FP8L
UNSPSC Code: 55101500

BISAC: BUSINESS & ECONOMICS / Leadership
Library of Congress Control Number: 2020912231

Editor: Dr. Rissy's Writing and Marketing

Illustrations by Shirin Abvabi
Audiobook narration by Robynne Orr

Dedication

I dedicate *What the Heck* to the daughters, mothers, sons, and fathers who had heroship thrust upon them but responded brilliantly.[1]
Heroes, such as Keedron Bryant, Johnetta "Netta" Elzi, Philonise Floyd, Darnella Frazier, Colin Rand Kaepernick, Lezley McSpadden, Darrell "Bubba" Wallace, Jr., and Rashad West come to mind.

In memory of Ahmaud Arbery and others…

7 Aiyana Jones
12 DeAunta Terrel Farrow
12 Tamir Rice
13 Andy Lopez
15 Jordan Edwards
15 Kiwane Carrington
16 Kimani Gray
17 Antwon Rose
17 Deion Fludd
17 Kwame "KK" Jones
17 Laquan McDonald
17 Trayvon Martin
17 Victor Steen
18 D'ettrick Griffin
18 Ervin Jefferson
18 Michael Brown, Jr.
18 Ramarley Graham
19 Christian Taylor
19 De'von Bailey
19 Kendrec McDade
19 Kenneth Harding
19 Quintonio LeGrier
19 Samuel David Mallard
19 Timothy Stansbury
19 Timothy Thomas
19 Tony Robinson
20 Brandon Webber
20 Danroy Henry
20 JaQuavion Slaton
20 Raheim Brown
20 Reynaldo Cuevas
20 Wendell Allen
20 Willie McCoy

21 Chavis Carter
21 Emantic "EJ" Bradford
21 Jimmy Atchison
21 Jonathan Hart
22 Jamee Johnson
22 John Crawford III
22 Oscar Grant
22 Rekia Boyd
22 Stephon Clark
22 Terrance Franklin
22 Victor White III
23 Amadou Diallo
23 Darius Tarver
23 DeAndre Ballard
23 Julius Johnson
23 Malcolm Ferguson
23 Miles Hall
23 Sean Bell
23 Shantel Davis
24 Akiel Denkins
24 Anthony Lamar Smith
24 Jamar Clark
24 Jonathan Ferrell
24 Maurice Granton
24 Ryan Twyman
25 Aaron Campbell
25 Dante Price
25 Ezell Ford
25 Freddie Gray
25 Kajieme Powell
25 McKenzie Cochran
25 Prince Jones
25 Reginald Doucet

26 Anthony Hill
26 Bothan Shem Jean
26 Breonna Taylor
26 Jamarion Robinson
26 Jemel Roberson
26 Jordan Baker
26 Mario Woods
26 Patrick Dorismond
26 Tarika Wilson
27 DeJuan Guillory
27 Rayshard Brooks
27 Sean Reed
27 Steven Eugene Washington
27 Tamon Robinson
28 Akai Gurley
28 Ariane McCree
28 Michael Dean
28 Orlando Barlow
29 Alonzo Ashley
29 Brendon Glenn
29 Nehemiah Dillard
30 Finan H. Berhe
30 Gregory Hill, Jr.
30 Malissa Williams
30 Shereese Francis
31 Christopher Whitfield
31 Dontre Hamilton
31 Henry Glover
31 Manuel Loggins, Jr.
31 Terrence Sterling
32 Larry Eugene Jackson, Jr.
32 Philando Castile
32 Phillip White

33 Manuel Ellis
33 Steven Demarco Taylor
34 Danny Ray Thomas
34 Miriam Carey
34 Raymond Allen
34 Rumain Brisbon
36 Dante Parker
36 Dellwood, Mo
36 Jerame Reid
36 Ronald Beasley
37 Alton Sterling
37 Derrick Jones
37 Tanisha Anderson
38 Alfred Olango
38 Natosha "Tony" McDade
38 Tony McDade
38 Tyree Woodson
40 Ronald Madison
40 Terence Crutcher
41 Robert Lawrence White
43 Carlos Alcis
43 Charly Keunang
43 Eric Garner
43 Johnnie Kamahi Warren
43 Keith Lamont Scott
43 Ousmane Zongo
43 Samuel DuBose
43 Timothy Russell
43 William Green
44 Eric Courtney Harris
46 George Floyd
47 Yassin Mohamed
47 Yvette Smith

49 Sharmel Edwards
49 Shem Walker
50 Patrick Harmon
50 Walter Scott
53 David McAtee

54 Eric Logan
57 Alberta Spruill
58 Gregory Gunn
68 Kenneth Chamberlain

From age seven to 68, this is a partial list of unarmed black Americans who have been killed by law enforcement. Each circumstance differs, but we should acknowledge the loss of life from the 141 families and extended families.

#7/68

Contents

Foreword xv
Preface xix
How Leadership Will Change Your Life 1
A Brief History of Leadership 5
What the Heck Is Management? 9
What the Heck Is Leadership? 15
You Need These to Lead 21
Do You Really Believe? 27
Forging the Links 37
Leadership Is Not about You 45
You Won't Succeed through Command and Control 49
Mistakes, Learning, and Growth 53
The Blame-Shift 61
Knowing about Leadership Is Not Enough 67
The Problem with Traditional Leadership 71
Epilogue: *What* and *Why* Do not Get You to *How* 75
Dedication Postscript 77
Acknowledgments 81
About the author 83
Endnotes 89

Foreword

Cultivating leadership, it's not about the resources you don't have; it's about resourcefulness! That is one of the first things my mentor Bill shared with me, and something Tony Robbins ingrained in me. Over a thirteen-year relationship with Bill, he shared many principals that he learned and used to build a mini-empire. When Bill started to take me under his wing and pass on his wisdom to me, one of the first things he shared was about personal leadership and why it is so important.

One of the ways Bill would teach me was to share a story then put me "behind the wheel," so I could experience the lesson. That was what he did when he shared the mindset he had and instilled in me. Bill put me behind the wheel of a blue corvette. Each time he shared a new lesson, he wanted me to **ABSORB** as much as I could, so the experience was ingrained not only in my head but in my heart and body. I am a visual learner, but he taught me to be able to learn through all my senses, so when times get tough, I could call on it in many ways. Tony Robbins calls that sensory acuity, and that is why I am so passionate about that topic and teach it. Great leaders all can ABSORB information quickly and put it to use.

In my book, *Moments Matter*, I write about the ability to **RESPOND** on the day of the Miracle on the Hudson. This was a driving force that enabled me to grow my business and succeed in life.

Building and reinforcing the **RESPOND** ability is critical to long-term success in any business. Demonstrating how your motives to support someone are genuine and congruent is the most effective way to build and reinforce responsiveness. Once people recognize that you have their best interest at heart, you gain their trust and rapport.

One of the things I noticed in my time with Tony Robbins and later around other top producers and leaders was something Bill told me he did. This one action helped him grow his business massively and, more importantly, helped him enjoy a 50+ year marriage to his wife, Bonnie. Bill would take time to **REFLECT** on what happened in a business project so he could fully comprehend the right, the wrong, and how to make progress.

After being on stage for three straight days for over 40 hours, Tony does the same thing: he shuts down and REFLECTS. Great leaders take the time to **REFLECT** on where they are and how they can add to their portfolio.

If you ever have been to or heard any of the great speakers from the '70's, 80's 90's and beyond, they all talk about the one thing that helped them get to where they are at is the ability to take **ACTION**. Bill told me the same thing. After he learned his 12 principals of business success from his mentor in the 1920s, the country and world went through the depression then a world war. There wasn't much optimism, and people were anxious. Bill told me he took massive action during the depression when people needed to see something positive, and motion pictures where just coming to age. If Bill didn't take **ACTION**, especially in a challenging time, he might never have become the entrepreneur that he was. The same with Jim Rohn, Tom Hopkins, and Tony Robbins. It is straight from the Bible: people who take massive ACTION get results and become leaders.

All the above are essential abilities to have. Still, Bill told me about another skill that exploded his business. This skill was his willingness to **SHARE** what he learned. In a time when people were trying to get an edge, money was tight, and the world was going to war, not many people wanted to reveal their knowledge. However, when they did share their insights, amazing things would happen. Think about the auto industry back in the '30s. The assembly line gave Henry Ford a significant advantage with the way he produced cars. Because he didn't keep the assembly line a secret, he impacted more industries than almost any other inventor. Bill shared his approach to growing in an evolving industry and improving. Reflecting on my actions, I found that when I strayed from what he told me, I struggled. Yet, when I followed his guidance, I became more effective in helping others grow.

Through stories, *What the Heck Is Leadership and Why Should I Care?* shares leadership concepts that, when taken individually or in whole, help you transform. First, through how to lead yourself, and then how to be an influential leader in your community and society.

Leaders often think they can control the future. Whenever I find myself counting on, or trying to control future events, especially right now, I'm reminded of the stories and lessons Gary shares. Gary shares these concepts with sincerity and a sense of humor that will keep you engaged. If you are open to absorb the lessons, respond to what you've learned, take a moment to reflect on how you can utilize the lesson to lead, then put it into action and most importantly, share it with others, you too can become the inspired leader you are meant to be. There is a lesson here for all of us.

Dave Sanderson
Best-selling author, philanthropist & survivor
of the Miracle on the Hudson plane crash

Preface

In 2015, CRC Press published my first book, *Nine Practices of 21st Century Leadership: A Guide for Inspiring Creativity, Innovation, and Engagement* or, for short, *Nine Practices*. This long-titled manuscript explains the radical evolution of leadership during the 21st century. *Nine Practices* has three parts: the *what* and *why* of leadership, *how to* practice it, and *how to* develop it. I include about one hundred leadership quotations from contemporary authors and performance-improvement experts to illustrate their harmonious insights developed from their unique experiences.

In *What the Heck Is Leadership and Why Should I Care?* Or, for short, *What the Heck*, I guide you through the progressive leadership elements to understand what they are.

A professional who adopts leadership, as I describe it, cultivates not just a healthier team, environment, and organization, but also has a healthier life.

Unlike *Nine Practices*, I employ a substantially different writing style. In *What the Heck*, you'll notice there's an absence of the typical tables, figure, callouts, and even bullet points. There are no inspirational leadership quotations, chapter summaries, or appendices. Instead of a bibliography, you'll find several endnotes like this one.[2]

What's blatant is an array of illustrations of cats with their young-adult caretaker—not what you typically see in a leadership book. The illustrator shares her abstract interpretation of the chapters' content.

If you're wondering why cats appear in a leadership book, I wouldn't be surprised. Since childhood, I've had them in my life. At first, I considered them as pets, but now I think I simply serve them. Serving others is a crucial ingredient of leadership.

In addition to cat illustrations, you'll discover *What the Heck* to be a narrative with a wealth of personal stories that reflect my leadership experiences. With some exceptions, I replace real names with fictitious ones in my recounts of life events. Of course, the same is true for fictional narratives, such as the two cashiers in Chapter 4.

In *Nine Practices*, I sourced fictional names from people I know to pay tribute to them. In *What the Heck*, I sourced some of the fictional first names from the 141 fallen Americans listed in the dedication. I also did this to honor them. When you read a name from one of my narratives, you might look at the dedication's list and then research their lives as a remembrance.

Here's the last difference between the two books. In *Nine Practices*, I use a deductive writing style in which I state a concept, describe it, share some examples, and maybe a couple of stories.

That's not the case in *What the Heck*. Instead, I mostly use an inductive style. I may start with some stories and then explain how they relate to a concept, such as one of the leadership principles.

Within these pages, I discuss serious leadership insights, but I do so with some humor and lightheartedness. I avoid academic jargon and even break from the formalness of the APA and Chicago style guides. Although these guides are so ingrained in my writing-DNA, I doubt I'll ever escape their influence, which is probably for the best.

As I write this, I realize that I'll soon be at the mercy of my editor. If this part of the preface makes the final cut, then you'll know that she has been merciful (I searched for a reliable editor, though, so we'll have to wait and see...or read).

So, free yourself of distractions and interruptions. Relax, and give your full attention to what you'll experience within bounds of this book. Please kindly enjoy.

Chapter 1

How Leadership Will Change Your Life

After graduate school, I managed cross-functional teams or was the senior employee on a team. Soon after, I started my first corporate management job.

Aiyana and I were a team of two. I was a thirty-something white manager, and Aiyana was a fifty-something performance engineer. We worked well together as a team, and I enjoyed my time with her. Although I may have been her manager, Aiyana led our team more than I did.

Aiyana's leadership had a lasting effect on my professional career. Without her, I wouldn't have sought my designation as a Certified Performance Technologist certification, and I wouldn't have become President of Tampa Bay ISPI. I wouldn't have known about this chapter if Aiyana hadn't asked me to attend some of their meetings. I also wouldn't have had the opportunity to speak at their events.

Devoid of my certification, I wouldn't have had the opportunity to facilitate a workshop that helped around 25 professionals work towards their certification. I also wouldn't have mentored younger professionals with their certification applications and career development. Most likely, I wouldn't have volunteered at the international level serving as the chair of the chapter partnership committee. If I hadn't served as the chair, I probably never would have met some of the most influential professionals who coached and mentored me. Without Aiyana's nudging, influence, and leadership, none of this would have happened.

Leadership enriches our lives. It has a powerful, cascading, and sustaining effect upon those we influence. With the right exposure, nudging, and support, those who lead can help us in our journey. They can inspire renewed confidence and help us realize extraordinary and unimagined opportunities that can change our lives for the better.

As we develop our leadership capabilities, our perceptions change. Interactions with direct reports, peers, and bosses become more meaningful and impactful. People notice our positive behaviors. They'll respect and trust us more, and equally, we develop more respect and trust in them. Through leadership, we become more fulfilled in what we do and, more so, as we evolve and grow this practice.

While problems and life challenges never cease, how these affect our spirit and attitude towards them won't be the same.

As we begin to lead in our workplaces, we experience some immediate results. First, those we lead feel more valued. Their encouragement grows as well as their desire to achieve their goals. Work becomes more enjoyable because of our interactions and renewed relationships. Bonds strengthen, and, if we're on a team, our teammates build camaraderie. Productivity and performance improve as the team tackles and reduces work barriers.

With time, changes continue. Our work environment improves. Teammates collaborate more frequently. Their outputs exhibit more creativity that results in innovations.

A couple of months ago, I started interviewing HR business partners for a public research report and another book. This month, I interviewed Ethan Crockett, a Strategic HR Business Partner for a national organization. During the interview, Ethan shared an experience he had in Roswell, Georgia, where he participated in a church group. The group created E3/L3 principles. Ethan explained to me how these principles guide him as he builds business and personal relationships.

Ethan defines E3 as *Encouraging, Equipping,* and *Experiencing* and L3 as *Living, Learning,* and *Leading*. These six actions are interconnected. For instance, learning results from leading, and leadership cannot happen without learning.

Although *leading* is an L3 principle, E3/L3 describes Ethan's overall leadership approach, which reflects his overwhelming accomplishments in helping business executives achieve their desired results.

Research studies found that emotions can be contagious. When we walk in a room full of people having fun and laughing, we're more likely to smile and even join in the fun. Like laughter, practicing leadership is contagious. When we lead, we model influential behaviors. Teammates will emulate our leadership practices, and even other teams will notice and begin to adopt our team's behaviors. Consciously or unconsciously, being influenced by leadership changes us for the better.

Leadership can affect communities in positive ways.

At another company, I worked for Rich Lima. Rich has accomplished a great deal during his career. He works hard to contribute to business goals and influence employee effectiveness. He has a knack for changing business for the better.

That success has manifested in how he helps his community. Serving on the board for the local Habitat for Humanity, Rich shares his business insights. He gives tenfold more than he gains.

For Rich and countless others, practicing leadership doesn't stop within the boundaries of an organization. Our work experiences affect our personal lives. Through the practice of leadership, society improves, and so do we. We volunteer our time and energy to serve those within our local and broader communities.

Leadership changes the lives of those around us and changes how we live our lives.

Here's my last point: leadership is not about me, you, or anyone who practices it. Leadership is about how we influence people and change their lives for the better.

Chapter 2

A Brief History of Leadership

Years ago, I completed a graduate-level leadership and management course, and here's what I remember from it: I think the textbook was green.

When taking a leadership course, a professor will introduce us to a bunch of theories, which are easy to teach. We'll learn about the Great Man Theory, Trait Theory, Contingency Theory, Transactional Theory, Transformational Theory, and so on. None of these helped me lead.

To be fair to professors, I didn't learn much because I had little interest in leadership or management while in graduate school. If someone traveled back in time and told me I would write leadership books, I wouldn't believe it. I'd also wonder why someone would waste time writing such a book.

Since graduate school, I've worked as an individual contributor, transitioned to management, and later became a manager of managers. Throughout those transitions, I relied on trial-and-error experimentation to develop how I managed and led.

My process changed after reading a book about servant leadership, which sparked my interest in leadership. That interest grew into a passion.

Forget about textbooks for a while. Let me share my layman's brief history of how leadership evolved. Maybe you'd prefer a $90 academic researched source, but for now, give this a try:

In the days of yore, we had leaders and followers. Those in charge, such as royalty, generals, company owners, and business partners, led. The rest followed.

Fast forward to the late 20th century (told you it was brief). Some smart people figured out that not only do those at the top lead, but anyone in management can lead as well. Supervisors, sergeants, principals, organizers, and of course, managers have a more direct connection with followers than at the top level. So, how management leads differs from how the top boss leads.

At the end of the 20th century, some experts started publishing books about an improved leadership approach. Concepts such as *Leading followers* became *serving followers*. Authors that come to mind include Stephen Covey, John C. Maxwell, and Ken Blanchard.

By the first decade of the 21st century, more authors, such as James Autry, Jim Collins, James Kouzes and Barry Posner, James C. Hunter, and Jason Jennings, contributed their insights to the leadership evolution.

By the second decade, some authors championed a radical idea: anyone, regardless of role, can practice leadership. Publications by Marshall Goldsmith, Liz Wiseman, Michael Abrashoff, Joseph

Grenny,[3] and David Marquet popularized this new leadership worldview.

In September of 2009, the leadership evolution congealed when TEDx posted an obscure video. This low-quality recording showed a young speaker in jeans (which became his signature style). He used a flip chart to explain what he called the world's simplest idea, the Golden Circle.

Simon Sinek's video has more than fifty million views, and translators have converted his talk into 48 languages.[4] A month after the TEDx post, Portfolio published Sinek's book, *Start with Why*.[5] In 2014, Sinek progressed his leadership insights in his book, *Leaders Eat Last*.[6]

When I've talked to others about leadership, I noticed that they tended to revert to traditional thinking. Some refer to their company's executive board as senior leadership. Others use the phrase "company leaders" to refer to their managerial levels. Either they imply that individual contributors don't lead, or they find it easier to lump these roles into one by calling them *leaders*.

Many professionals have accepted that leadership isn't the same as management. More and more, I'm finding organizations training their employees in non-managerial roles to lead.

So, if management is not the same as leadership, then what the heck does *management* mean? Read on.

Chapter 3

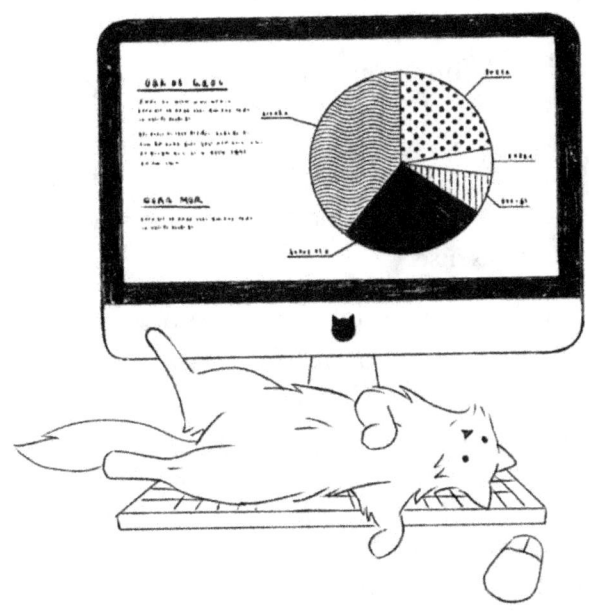

What the Heck Is Management?

As mentioned earlier, I was managing teams for several years. Before and since my last corporate job, I've met some brilliant executives, directors, and managers. From the armed forces, I've become acquainted with some extraordinary officers as well. I've been fortunate to mostly work with and associate with exceptionally talented managers at all career levels. If you read Liz Wiseman's debut leadership book, you might label these professionals as multipliers.[7]

However, I've worked with some managers who give new meaning to behaving narcissistically. You might label them as diminishers. I didn't get along with diminishers, and they would eventually send me away with a lengthy contract to keep me quiet. That stated, of all the managers I knew, maybe I would consider one in twenty to practice the dark side of management.

One thing that drives me nuts is reading or watching videos of *experts* who proclaim to have the answer about how leadership and management differ. While some of their explanation might have a semblance of truth, too often, they get it wrong.

In one video, an expert associates management with being smart and having a high IQ while leadership is about having a high EQ. This argument is nonsense!

IQ is an acronym for Intelligence Quotient, but some are unaware that EQ is an acronym for Emotional Quotient. Most refer to EQ as emotional intelligence. Expecting a creative answer, I asked Coachsultant Peter Popovich for a simple way to think about EQ, and here's what he came up with:

"EQ is two bottles of RUM: Recognize, Understand, and Manage our emotions (first bottle) and then Recognize, Understand and Manage the emotions of others (second bottle). RUM Squared (RUM)^2 increases our intelligence, options, and happiness!"[8] Now when I think of RUM, I think of emotional intelligence…and Peter.

The worst experts offer this message: "Leadership equals good. Management equals bad." Even Sinek, whose insights into leadership I highly regard, defines management as "the manipulation of others for personal gain."[9] When I searched the Internet for *management vs. leadership*, the search query read someone like the promotion for a boxing match between the heavyweight champion, *management*, against the underdog, *leadership*.

Here is more nonsense: some experts explain that management is about maintaining the status quo.

To be fair, though, management hasn't always been perceived positively. From a historical perspective, managers and workers have had an adversarial relationship. Around the middle of the 19th century, employees formed labor unions to counter social and economic hardships brought on by the Industrial Revolution. During that time, companies used management as a tool to maximize productivity at the expense of their labor force.

Regardless of the historical perspective, describing management as bad is a red herring—a misleading clue. Think of management as analogous to money. People use both for doing good or evil acts. It's unfortunate when many use managers tactically to achieve objectives at the expense of their people. Too often, they do this while proclaiming that human capital is their most valued asset within their company.

While management is neither good nor bad, understanding what management is helps clarify what leadership isn't, and leadership ain't management!

Management is a formal role consisting of well-defined tasks. I separate management into four categories: managers of organizations, processes, projects, and people.

The categories aren't exclusive in the sense that managers functions within only one type. At one company, I ran the training department, and my role performed within the last three categories. For example, when I worked with executives to form my department, I defined and managed the processes. I also managed several projects and the team as well.

Managers tend to have individual contributor tasks. At one company's call center, supervisors managed agents but also handled escalated calls. Supervisors tended to be highly experienced subject-matter experts whom the director promoted from their pool of call-center agents.

Here's another example of how these supervisors functioned as individual contributors. When developing training, my team leveraged their expertise. With the director's approval, supervisors collaborated to create and test call-center training.

Geary Rummler, whom Roger Addison and Carol Haig describe as the Performance Architect's Architect, writes about three managerial responsibilities.[10] First, they set the goals. For example, a CEO is responsible for organizational strategies.

Next, they design. A CEO is accountable for creating the structure of business units and departments; the CEO also owns assigning the process responsibilities to each group.

Finally, managers monitor and adjust, which Rummler calls, job management. A CEO does this by modifying organizational goals to redirect resources to respond to a competitor's threat.

Rummler's three responsibilities apply to each of the four managerial categories. For example, project managers ensure that the project has goal clarity. Using work plans and Work Breakdown Structure (WBS), they design how the team will execute the project. As the project progresses, project managers monitor the tasks. If plans or circumstances change, they adjust the scope, timeline, and resources, as needed.

Managers of people tend to share everyday tasks. For example, managers approve worker requests and conduct performance reviews. They assign work to their direct reports and monitor progress.

One of my least desired tasks was firing and reducing my workforce. During one substantial workforce reduction at one company, I laid off one of my teams. The only good that came from this was persuading my boss to reassign the team's manager to an individual contributor role in another department. The manager accepted her new position and was happy for the change and the opportunity to use her creativity more effectively than in her previous role.

To recap, management is a formal role that involves setting goals, designing the area of responsibility, monitoring that area, and adapting to the changing environment.

One more thing: Mary Parker Follett, a pioneer in the field of organizational design, defined management as "the art of getting things done through people."[11] I used to think that this was a leadership definition. It isn't. An essential part of management is accomplishing tasks through others.

Consider managers of people: a manager directs and monitors work but doesn't do the actual work (not meaning that managers don't work).

Directing others to do the work is a monumental challenge for managers. Many work on tasks that they should assign to direct reports. Others complete tasks because the effort to explain and coach direct reports takes longer than just doing it themselves.

The manager fallacy is failing to recognize that training direct reports to do these tasks gradually increases the employees' value to the organization while reducing the often-overburdened managers' workload.

If management is a formal role and involves getting tasks accomplished through others, then what the heck is leadership?

Chapter 4

What the Heck Is Leadership?

At one of the companies where I worked, people at all career levels modeled leadership behaviors. Senior management spent a substantial amount of dollars, time, and effort promoting leadership and how to practice it.

I remember receiving job aids that explained expected leadership habits. For example, we should model fairness and approachability. We should remove obstacles that interfered with teaming and inclusiveness. When listening to someone's opinion or idea, we should be open to new ways of thinking without assuming that we already know what's best.

The company discouraged certain behaviors. For example, we should stop resisting experimentation. We shouldn't show favor towards others who think and act similarly. We also shouldn't strengthen a group at the expense of other groups and the company.

Such behaviors were the antithesis of leading.

Not everyone practiced leadership. Some knew the words but didn't live by them. Regardless, the company invested in developing everyone's leadership capabilities. While I was working there, my curiosity about leadership grew.

When I discuss leadership, I avoid using the word, leader. I associate *leader* with traditional thinking, which I describe in Chapter 13. Whether it was because of the evolution of leadership, the company's culture, or larger company size, I met fewer traditionalists during my time there than at other companies.

In the previous chapter, I described management as a formal role that involves getting things done through others. Leadership is not that.

On job boards, you might see such titles as *team lead* or *project leader*. The armed forces also include *leader* in some of their ranks. Don't be fooled. These are different ways to label the supervisor and project manager roles. Some may have a certain amount of responsibility for directing others but without anyone directly reporting to them.

At an international company, I functioned as a team lead for an international team of trainers. I participated in regular conference calls and collaborated with trainers to create deliverables that the team could use at their home office. Doing so eliminated a substantial amount of duplication.

The trainers didn't report to me. They didn't even have to attend the calls. Some might say that the trainers had a dotted line that linked to me, but none appeared under me in any organizational charts.

Having been in human resources, I've read several job descriptions. In a few, I've seen task responsibilities such as "lead a team" or "act as a leader for direct reports." These vague tasks are synonymous with managing rather than practicing leadership.

When practicing leadership, we realize that those we influence also influence us. Colleagues have shared that when they coach or mentor others, they learn and grow as much or more than their recipients.[12] This is the first element of leadership: it is bidirectional. Management is not.

When I've consulted with companies, some shared a list of manager competencies or qualities. The companies typically included the word, *leadership*. Leadership isn't a competency, but it encompasses several skills that contribute to leading effectively.

Leadership isn't a work process, but it involves a set of actions that are derived from principles. These repeatable acts, what I call *practices*, enhance work processes. Practices produce more favorable outcomes and influence how people around us behave. Practices can even strengthen organizational culture.

Roger Addison is an author and performance consultant who has years of experience facilitating workshops and training professionals. I still learn from Roger, and we keep in touch.

During one of his workshops, Roger explained the distinction between process and practice. Anyone involved in Six Sigma, Kaizen, or Lean Manufacturing should learn this distinction.

To explain the difference, Roger shared the following story:

Imagine that you are a process detective. Today, at a small grocery store, you observe two cashiers: Yvette and Sean. In your hand is a copy of the store's process documentation, and your objective is to reference the document to confirm that Yvette and Sean comply with the process steps.

After watching them perform several transactions, you conclude that both complete the steps as described in the documentation. However, you notice something unusual: Yvette's customer line is longer than Sean's.

Even though both stations are identical, customers seem to prefer Yvette's station. For example, customers choose to stand in Yvette's longer line than switching to Sean's shorter one for a faster purchase.

Watching both cashiers, you discover the difference. While both greet customers with a smile (required in the process), Yvette greets customers by name. She even seems to know her customers well.

While scanning merchandise, Yvette asks customers about their day and comments about items they are purchasing, but not in a judgmental or offensive way. She asks how they have enjoyed past purchases and lets them know about new promotions that are coming soon. As customers take their groceries, Yvette expresses how she appreciates seeing them again.

Both cashiers thank customers as required, but Yvette does so in a way that resonates with them.

Both cashiers are sincere, pleasant, and efficient, but Yvette practices the checkout process differently than Sean.

From this example, employees can perform the same process with the desired outcome. Without deviating from the steps, some achieve better results.

In the cashier example, customers who complete their purchases with Yvette have a better experience than customers with Sean (no offense, Sean).

Think of *process* as a series of behaviors that achieve predictable results and *practice* to enhance the process by integrating personal mannerisms, habits, and in some instances, customs.

If you can accept that leadership involves a set of practices and isn't a role, you might argue that this doesn't explain what the heck leadership is. Well, fair enough.

When we lead, we influence others to change. Specifically,

leadership practices enable us to help others mature their mental and moral qualities, capabilities, and behaviors. That's the formal way to define leadership: helping others build character.

L. David Marquet explains that leadership is not about getting others to do stuff. That's management. Instead, leadership is about getting people to think. Thus, leadership is not about you but other people. It's about creating a work environment in which people can be at their best.[13]

While captain of the Santa Fe, a nuclear submarine, Marquet experimented with leading. His goal was to transform his crew from following to leading. In other words, he wanted more leadership and less followership.

For his crew to develop their leadership capabilities, he needed them to think for themselves while not worrying about making mistakes or fretting about what the chain of command would do. If in doubt, the crew could explain their intent to their chief. The chief might ask questions to get them thinking or to build their confidence. Instead of ordering the crew member to execute the task, the chief would then ask the sailor to carry on.

The Santa Fe's crew transformed because Marquet changed the submarine's working environment.[14]

Not only did Marquet transform his crew and turn the ship around, but the crew also led one another to achieve goal after goal. The results were brilliant!

Chapter 5

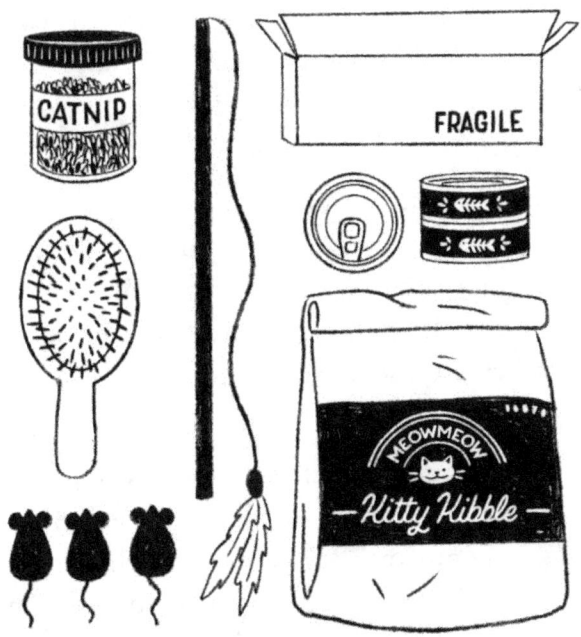

You Need These to Lead

Have you ever been in a staff meeting in which no one talked but the manager? That was Brendon's challenge.

Every week, Brendon would meet with his team. Each time, he'd review the agenda and then discuss company and department updates. At some point, he'd ask the team to share their opinion and ask for feedback. This didn't happen.

Brendon envisioned engaging in a healthy dialogue. The team would reveal what was and wasn't working and then figure out how to fix it. Brendon would later explain that this is what he thought healthy teams did. They would agree, disagree, debate, and resolve. For Brendon, these behaviors would enable them to become a high-performing team.

Sadly, Brendon's reality differed. To start this exchange, Brendon would ask for their thoughts, such as how effectively the team tackled recent tasks. Inevitably, the team had two behavioral patterns. Most of the time, no one would speak. After waiting for what felt like minutes with no response, Brendon would change the subject and move on to other topics.

Other times, someone would comment. Brendon's hopes would rise but only momentarily. After commenting, Brendon would encourage others to join in the conversation. Instead, the team would look down at their notepads or avoid eye contact. Everyone seemed uncomfortable, including Brendon.

Brendon knew that he needed help. After he shared his problem with me, I asked Brendon a few questions and came to three observations. First, although he was knowledgeable about the business and his company, Brendon never thought much about leadership. Second, Brendon sincerely wanted to achieve his vision of leading a high-performing team. Third, Brendon tried several tactics to engage his team but without success. From these observations, I uncovered what prevented Brendon from leading effectively.

Before explaining this, you need to know something about Brendon.

Before supervising his team, Brendon worked as a programmer in a technology development team of programmers. The teammates worked independently but consulted with one another and shared programming insights.

What Brendon mostly did was spend hours struggling with code. For him, he found that the work was more than educational—it was rewarding! Through his work, Brendon discovered creative solutions and was thrilled to share his breakthroughs with his teammates.

When I talked with Brendon, he didn't realize how little he knew about leadership. What he knew about leaders came from his interactions with executives and managers. He spent most of his time with Breonna, his team's manager, and picked up a few of her leadership habits.

I asked Brendon to describe his leadership approach. For the first time, he had to think about what leadership is and how he approached it. Even though Breonna and other managers modeled leading, Brendon had trouble explaining to me what they did and why.

When I asked him how his teammates led, he didn't understand or even fathom that teammates could effectively lead without having managerial authority. This concept was foreign to him.

Brendon found leadership to be challenging for two reasons. When watching Breonna and other managers, Brendon didn't know how to separate their managerial behaviors from their leadership practices.

More importantly, Brendon couldn't observe the principles that guided how managers led.

Think of Brendon's problem this way: I can see someone's behavior, but I can't observe why people behave the way they do. That's why criminal prosecutors have difficulty convincing juries to rule a defendant as guilty of first-degree murder. To do so, prosecutors would have to infer intent to plan as well as execute the act.

Determining why people lead the way they do is difficult, but even more so is figuring out leadership principles. Learning what a principle is and then seeing examples would be much easier than finding behavioral patterns that lead to principles used to guide behaviors for different situations.

Earlier, I shared that leadership is a way of practicing our roles. *Principles* guide how we lead. If we can internalize leadership principles so we can apply them to different types of situations, we can lead effectively. Unfortunately, as the phrase goes, this is easier said than done.

You may wonder if principles and values are the same. I tend to lump values with qualities, competencies, skills, abilities, and traits. Values are more abstract than principles. Examples of values are honesty, courage, selflessness, and humility.

Principles are more specific. For example, I know several consultants who work from the Add-Value Principle: deliver to clients more than what they pay you. Clients benefit greatly from this principle, but consultants do so as well.

Because values are so abstract, I find it hard to learn leadership by only studying leadership values. Even more challenging is identifying what leadership values are. On LinkedIn, I found three lengthy discussions in which moderators asked group members to describe leadership qualities. I made a list of all the values that members shared. After eliminating duplicates, I listed 270 qualities!

I avoid the challenge of identifying values by focusing on *principles* instead.

Leadership principles are specific enough to explain how to apply them but abstract enough to apply to many types of situations. Think of leadership principles as our moral compass that guides us through turbulent and calm waters. The more we internalize the principles, the better we lead.

While leadership principles are more useful than values or qualities, few leadership experts have a comprehensive list of principles. To be fair about my argument for not using values, experts don't agree on a standard set of principles. When it comes to leadership, there's no ISO 9000.

To identify leadership principles for my book, *Nine Practices*,[15] I analyzed fourteen books written by leadership experts. All but one were published in the twenty-first century. From these books, I identified seven leadership principles. In the next seven chapters, I'll introduce you to each one.

Chapter 6

Do You Really Believe?

Tony is a VP who hired me to lead a small team. The team included DeAunta and Miles. Tony wanted me to fire them. Later, I discovered that Tony hired me because I had experience firing employees, while other candidates didn't.

I asked Tony what DeAunta and Miles had done and why he hadn't fired them already. In response, he described the two as lazy and disruptive. When walking by their workspace, Tony observed them searching the web, balancing their checkbook, or talking to other employees who were trying to work. Seldom did he see them working on company projects.

To answer my second question, Tony wanted someone else to collect evidence to fire them, and that "someone else" was me. Because Tony didn't work directly with DeAunta and Miles, he had some doubts as to whether he was right or not.

After spending some time with them, I quickly realized that both employees were smart and insightful. They shared insights into the department and the corporate culture. They even helped me navigate some of the politics and provided accurate insights into the strengths and challenges of our department.

Relevant to Tony's observations, I discovered that DeAunta and Miles were bored and didn't have enough work.

Management added to the problem by delaying draft reviews of their deliverables. I evaluated one of the larger projects but couldn't figure out why the deliverable wasn't approved and implemented. I asked Tony about the delayed review. In return, he asked if I found anything wrong with it. No. He then told me to implement the deliverable.

It turns out that management counted on-hold projects as part of the employees' active workload. Because DeAunta and Miles were sitting with nothing to do and waiting for work, they had to find ways to spend their time.

I ensured that DeAunta and Miles had plenty of meaningful work to accomplish. They agreed to let me know when they didn't have enough to do so they could stay productive.

DeAunta and Miles both did fantastic work. After I left the organization, I learned that management promoted DeAunta twice. At the same time, Miles continued to excel in the same role. Both survived several workforce reductions and still work in the same department.

Here's the point: When I started working with DeAunta and Miles, I didn't assume that they were lazy. Instead, I worked from the premise that they were decent people and believed in them.

What gave Tony a negative perception had nothing to do with their character but everything to do with a problematic circumstance caused by a flawed process.

Whether we're owners of a company, managers, or teammates, we influence those around us and shape our environment for better or for worse. Likewise, the explicit and tacit beliefs we have about others affect their ability to contribute and succeed in their jobs.

To lead others effectively, we need to shape our thoughts deliberately. Doing so enables us to follow the first principle of leadership: *Believe in Others.*

Carol Dweck, a pioneer in motivational research, has helped millions of professionals change how they think about themselves and others. She champions the idea that we can develop our thinking and reasoning continuously.

The research concludes that intelligence is not static but dynamic. In Dweck's book, *Mindset*, and TEDx talk, she explains two mindsets that shape how we perceive our environment and interact with others.[16]

Think of these two mindsets as how we view ourselves and how this self-perception affects the way we live our lives. A mindset consists of a set of conscious or unconscious beliefs. These beliefs shape our perceptions of our abilities and habits. They also influence how we perceive others.

Susan works as a technician at a pharmaceutical company. She's been in the role for seven years and wants to become a supervisor with more responsibilities and better pay.

Before her shift starts, Orlando, her manager, takes Susan aside and tells her that he decided to give the supervisory position to Samuel instead of her. Susan wanted this promotion, and as you might expect, she was disappointed and sad. After her shift, Susan shared her news with Rekia, a close friend. Rekia asked, "How do you feel?"

How would you feel? What thoughts go through your mind? How would you move forward knowing that you'll return to work and see Samuel supervising the technicians you thought you'd be managing? Enter the two mindsets.

Suppose Susan responded, "I feel like a loser." She might go on to say, "Orlando chose Samuel because he likes him more" or "Someone in the corporate office doesn't like me" or "I'm a total failure." What did Susan do? She drank some wine, went to bed early, and then went back to work, expecting that if she applied for another job, she wouldn't have a chance.

Susan's reaction is from a fixed mindset. When we think using this mindset, we believe that our intelligence, traits, and abilities are set in stone or *fixed*. Believing that these are fixed in adulthood leads to thoughts such as: "I can't draw." "Michael Jordan is a gifted athlete."[17] "I'm not as smart as others think." "Failing is harmful."

Dweck makes an interesting point about people who think from a fixed mindset; they urgently want to prove to others—and themself—that they aren't deficient in IQ, EQ, traits, and abilities.

We don't start life with a fixed mindset. We develop it because of how people treat us. If we receive an A on a paper, and our parents and friends describe us as smart, we slowly move towards a fixed mindset.

Being told that we are smart sets the expectation that we will behave smartly, which builds the desire to prove we're smart, even if we don't feel it. Think about how much worse children might feel when scoring low on a test while knowing that others expect them to be smart. The experience can cause a considerable amount of unwarranted pressure.

Like telling children they're smart, labeling managers as leaders has the same effect. The leader expectation can become a burden when managers don't perceive themselves as leaders, especially for those new to management who already have some doubts about their capabilities.

Briefly, I worked for Renea, a VP who came to the company from a different industry and without much experience. Renea self-inflicted the leadership expectation on herself by telling others that she is a leader of people. From the employee viewpoint, she didn't seem to model leadership but command and control. Renea seldom showed that she enjoyed her role.

Renea wasn't a bad person, but she did seem to struggle to maintain her leadership façade. Renea never explained what being a leader meant, but she did send an implicit message for employees were to serve her. Renea is no longer with the company.

When we think from a fixed mindset, we exhibit behaviors such as avoiding difficult tasks. We laugh when others appear foolish and then spread rumors to make others look less favorable while implying that we are better than them.

Instead of reacting from a fixed mindset, what if Susan responded differently when Rekia asked her how she felt and what she would do next. In this scenario, Susan answers, "Even though I'm disappointed, I know that some supervisor positions will be available soon. When Orlando posts the next requisition, I'll be the first to apply!" Her response is a far cry from feeling like a failure and being stuck in a role.

In the revised scenario, Susan's reaction comes from a growth mindset. When we view life through this mindset, we think and act as if we can develop and improve our IQ, EQ, traits, abilities, and competencies. Believing that adults can continue to grow leads to thoughts such as: "Taking an art class can help me learn to draw." "Michael Jordan's dedication to practice and learning led to his remarkable achievements."[18] "I still can improve how smart I am." "Failing is a fantastic way to learn and improve."

When we think from a growth mindset, we exhibit behaviors such as working diligently to solve a problem, asking the boss for a stretch assignment, seeking a peer for help, and giving others credit for their contributions.

Try this: I'm going to share six statements, and I'd like for you to decide if you agree, somewhat agree, somewhat disagree, or disagree. Here's they are:

1. When people achieve significant accomplishments, it isn't a good idea to tell them how smart they are.
2. Hiring candidates who are fully qualified for jobs makes more sense than hiring candidates who meet core requirements but are partially qualified.
3. When I experience a setback, I may feel discouraged or disappointed before I try again.
4. Some professionals are natural leaders.
5. The people I work with have a lot of potential at improving their performance.
6. Although I may not admit it, I sometimes envy a peer's promotion when I'm more qualified.

Each statement represents the thinking from either a fixed or growth mindset.

The first statement is from a growth mindset. I'll explain with an example from Dweck's childhood.[19]

Mrs. Wilson's sixth-grade class was unique. She believed that the IQ of her students established their intelligence level and character. High IQ equals good. Low IQ equals bad.

Mrs. Wilson took this concept to the next level. She assigned student's seats in the order of their IQ scores. At one end of the classroom were students with the highest IQ, and the other end sat students with lower IQ scores. There's more. As Dweck explains it, Mrs. Wilson trusted only students with the highest IQs to take on privileged tasks such as carrying the American flag. From Mrs.

Wilson's way of thinking, students with a lower IQ couldn't be dependable to take notes to the principal's office and promptly return. In her class, she changed the broad aim of school from learning to appearing smart while not looking foolish.

Instead of praising intelligence, try praising effort. Avoid praising IQ, talent-level, and gifted abilities. Try saying, "You studied a great deal before the test, and look what you accomplished! You reviewed your notes, you outlined what could be on the test, and you even asked yourself test questions. That really worked for you!" In her book, Dweck has a chapter devoted to assisting parents, teachers, and coaches in promoting the growth mindset.

The second statement is from a fixed mindset. If a hiring manager told a job applicant that she made the job offer because the candidate is a superstar and expects terrific accomplishments, imagine the pressure the applicant would experience when making her first mistake. Also, the hiring manager's statement implies that the candidate does not need to develop while in this role.

Early in my career, I discovered a hiring secret. If I hired less experienced candidates who still meet the core requirements, two things would happen. First, new hires perform better than predicted. Second, they would have plenty of room to grow and want to develop while in the role.

In their book, *Nuts!*, Freiberg and Freiberg eloquently explain that when others believe in us, they help us grow, mature, and become more capable.[20] When selecting a candidate, make clear how you want your new hire to develop and learn.

The third statement is from a growth mindset. When our plans fail to materialize, we naturally can experience disappointment. What differentiates growth and fixed mindsets is how we respond to setbacks.

The fourth statement is from a fixed mindset. Believing that natural leaders exist is another way of thinking that we are born with certain traits, as well as with a set IQ and EQ.

The fifth statement is from a growth mindset. When I worked in corporations, I experienced the opposite when the managers discussed performance reviews. Some managers had given up with some employees. In their minds, these employees couldn't improve. The managers simply stopped believing in them.

By the way, ranking employees from highest to lowest during performance reviews is another way of reinforcing a fixed mindset. Performance rankings can become a substantial distraction and productivity killer, which is the opposite of the review's intent.

The last one is a fixed-mindset statement that should remind you of Susan's situation.

Here are some critical points about fixed and growth mindsets. First, the concepts are easy to grasp but harder to recognize when we're using a fixed or growth mindset. We often react or respond to situations without considering which mindset is influencing our current behavior.

Second, our mindset can shift frequently. As circumstances and environments change, our mindset may change as well. When I'm tired, I could start thinking from a fixed mindset. Moments later, I might recognize what's happening and shift back to a growth mindset.

People tend to be a mix of the two. Some may tend to be stuck in a fixed mindset but have instances when they think from a growth mindset. The reverse is also true.

Next, deciding that certain people have either a fixed or growth mindset is another way to label them—classic fixed mindset thinking!

In her research, Dweck discovered that companies could trend towards fixed or growth mindsets. Her research reveals that a company's mindset affects the likelihood that employees would behave in particular ways.

In Harvard Business Review, the authors found that companies that nurture a growth mindset employ people who are 47 percent more likely to perceive colleagues as being trustworthy. They also are 34 percent more likely to feel a strong sense of ownership and commitment towards their company. 65 percent are more inclined to say that their company supports risk-taking, and 49 percent are more willing to say that their company fosters innovation.[21]

One last point: Raising our awareness about fixed and growth mindsets helps us shift our thinking toward a growth mindset. Hilary Scarlett, the author of *Neuroscience for Organizational Change*, explains that doing so could strengthen team engagement, improve the team's health, and increase performance. Doing so would also enhance our belief in others.[22]

If we believe in others, and I mean really believe, then good things will come. That's not just my opinion. Researchers have proven that this phenomenon is real.

Chapter 7

Forging the Links

At a company where I worked, the chief HR officer assigned Randy Moon as the SVP of Learning and Organizational Effectiveness, a department of about 90 employees. On the day of the change, we gathered in an amphitheater for Randy to address his new employees.

After the formal niceties, Randy began to speak. Instead of talking about a vision or what he wanted the department to accomplish, he spoke about his life and family but then shared an unusual story.

After helping a company in Buenos Aires, Randy left the building to return to his hotel. When he entered what appeared to be a taxi, he found himself among kidnappers. They had abducted him, but for whatever reason, they eventually released him.

When business plans don't work out, some employees become upset. Not Randy. Being kidnapped in Argentina has strengthened his tolerance and lowered his stress levels—Randy doesn't sweat the small stuff anymore.

The kidnapping story isn't my point, but the effect the story had on employees is.

Afterward, I talked with a few colleagues about the meeting. Most didn't know Randy but had seen him in the building. What I found rememberable was how they expressed their admiration for Randy and looked forward to talking with him after he moved to his new office.

Randy's introduction and story established a profound connection even though Randy personally didn't know the employees who had only worked under him for a few hours. They trusted Randy.

Remember Brendon in Chapter 5? Brendon had trouble getting direct reports to talk during team meetings. Here's what I hadn't shared: while his team liked Brendon, they didn't trust him or feel comfortable speaking their mind.

Contrast Brendon's experience with Randy's. Employees wanted to meet and get to know Randy, which they did. Randy's door was open most of the time, and he honestly enjoyed it when people walked in and chat. I did so as well.

For a consulting project at a national organization, I had facilitated several focus groups with employees to learn about how managers led their teams. Similarly, I interviewed managers to learn how their VPs led their management teams.

During the group interviews, some employees expressed that they didn't openly share their opinions and perspectives with their bosses. One said, "When I was honest, my director threw a fit. That was the last time I warned him about a cultural issue." Another wouldn't give his manager feedback. He explained, "I didn't want to hurt his feelings, so I said that everything's fine." Another complained that as soon as he would voice a concern, his boss ruthlessly belittled her opinion. "He was relentless," she sighed. "Brent described these conversations as 'healthy talks' that set things straight. I thought of them as a mental beating."

Amy C. Edmondson, Harvard professor and author of *The Fearless Organization*, sounded the alarm for organizations to adopt psychological safety.[23] According to Edmondson, there is a fundamental truth about organizational life: we cannot know when someone is withholding their thoughts. If we observe someone being silent or hear an employee saying that everything's okay, we can either accept what they say or guess their intent. Likewise, we can't always know by looking at employees when they are overwhelmed with a problem or don't know how to complete a task.

Too frequently, we incorrectly guess what others are thinking. If you understand the Fundamental Attribution Error, you know what I mean.

Edmondson's fundamental truth calls us out: we can observe behaviors, but we can only guess intent. Instead, we can encourage others to share their thoughts. Enter Edmondson's psychological safety.[24] When we believe that we can safely take interpersonal risks without fear of scorn or animosity, we experience psychological safety.

I admire how Patrick Lencioni describes what happens when we feel safe among a team.[25] When this happens, we can genuinely say things like, "I made a mistake." "I need help." "I was wrong." "Your idea is better than mine." "I wish I could learn how to do that as well as you."

In her research, Edmondson found that psychological safety encourages behavioral changes among teammates. Behaviors such as sharing ideas, asking for feedback, and discussing problems happen more frequently.

As these behaviors become habits, they increase the amount of experimentation, innovation, learning, and engagement.

How do we create this safe environment for our team, colleagues, groups, and family? We *Connect with Others*, which is the second leadership principle.

Think about Randy's kidnapping and how his willingness to share resulted in employees liking and engage with him.

When we share what's happened in our lives, especially our mistakes and imperfections, others become more open with their mistakes. By being vulnerable, we create a path for others to express their vulnerability.

Vulnerability builds trust. Being vulnerable is like saying, "I'll share my shortfalls with you, and I trust that you won't use them against me."

When I started my first management job, I didn't know about psychological safety. I had read that bosses shouldn't be friends with employees. If bosses become too friendly, they risk being partial and biased. I wish I hadn't fallen prey to that belief. Not building friendships with direct reports is a managerial mistake and a flawed traditional leadership assumption.

Here's something else that I learned from Simon Sinek: having a work-life balance is not about having a balance between the time spent working compared to the time off the clock. It's about being emotionally healthy at work as well as at home.

When work difficulties upset us or cause stress, we take those feelings home with us. Likewise, what happens at home affects how we behave at work. We're human and can't effectively compartmentalize what happens in our personal lives from our professional lives and vice versa.

Southwest Airlines has figured this out.[26] When a family member is admitted to intensive care, Southwest knows that the employees cannot work well while worrying about a loved one. So, Southwest makes sure that employees spend time with their hospitalized family members. They send flowers and check in with how employees are doing. They make sure that the hospital takes care of everyone and contributes as well.

Having a difficult time concentrating at work doesn't apply to just family emergencies. Events around the world can profoundly affect our wellbeing. On September 11, 2001, a friend called me at work about a plane that crashed into one of the towers at the World Trade Center. I stopped what I was doing and went to her house. There, I watched the towers fall. The effect was immediate and powerful. I still recall what that felt like knowing that people were dying senselessly. Returning to work that day didn't happen.

Like the World Trade Center, the world recently witnessed how a brave teenager with a video camera captured a police officer murdering George Floyd. With his hands in his pockets, the man in blue pressed his knee into this father's neck for eight minutes and forty-six seconds. Floyd was black—the officer white.

This horrifying event shocked and angered millions. Our hearts went out to this man and to the family who had their lives turned upside down. When we experience such an unjust loss, we cannot view the world in the same way. How surreal it is watching others go about their lives and seeing normalcy when such evil has happened.

But life didn't go on as it usually does when a story breaks about another unarmed black man dying at the hands of police.

While this isn't the first video documenting police murdering unarmed black men, this was different. What happens exceeded anything that Hollywood or video games could produce.

Floyd's repeated pleading, the begging of bystanders, the lack of empathy and care from the three assisting officers, the casualness and indifference of the murderer, and the unendurable duration was enough to expose our nation for what it has become. White people could not look away without being affected and, finally, look at the excessive oppression of their brothers and sisters of a different race.

Yes, this was different. Without the bravery of a teenager and merchant who made sure the world witnessed this reality, this would have been just the continuation of an unanswered act of injustice and unwarranted dehumanization.

People could not watch the news without experiencing the outcry. The media documented the wave after wave of international protests that manifested through peaceful marches but with some property destruction coupled with looting. As Americans, we watched how our government reacted, and we saw the good with the bad.

Something else was different. Whites and blacks marched together. Many government officials supported and even joined protests. Within two weeks of Floyd's death, corporate America responded as well. Several CEOs and owners wrote employees and their customers to condemn the killing.[27] The Carolina Panthers NFL team broke ties with CPI Security after the CEO made racist comments.[28] Michael Jordan donated $100 million to support social justice organizations.[29] During a CNN interview, Darrell "Bubba" Wallace, Jr., the only black driver at NASCAR's top level, asked NASCAR to ban Confederate flags from their sporting events. NASCAR did.

I could go on and on, and I know that my account is lacking and doesn't sufficiently describe everything that's happening. With Floyd's death just fifteen days ago, the narrative continues to develop.

There's a point I want to get to, but I need to share another story.

In 2012, the media reported how George Zimmerman shot and killed an unarmed 17-year-old. The young man's name was Trayvon Martin. As with Floyd, people protested throughout the United States. Unlike with Floyd, white Americans didn't express their outrage and probably wouldn't recognize Martin's name when mentioned a month later.

When Zimmerman murdered Trayvon Martin, I don't recall any CEOs writing public letters denouncing Martin's murder. Management didn't talk to employees about it. Maybe I missed it, but I don't remember anyone openly discussing what happened. I know that black employees were affected, but I didn't talk with my fellow HR colleagues, who were black.

Compared to what's being discussed now, 2012 is a stark contrast. We could have done more. I could have done better.

Our imagination and compassion can only take us so far, but for what happened to George Floyd, watching that video didn't require imagination.

Writer tiffany dockery, who spells her name without capital letters, explains that white people may not know what to do or say when these murders occur.[30] Asking our black colleagues if they're doing okay may not be helpful. Of course, they aren't okay under these circumstances.

Instead of asking if someone is okay, dockery recommends making a statement. Just saying, "You don't have to respond, but I want you to know I'm here for you if you want someone to listen to you." Small acts of kindness can be more meaningful to someone than we realize.

While privately consoling someone may help, dockery recommends taking a stance to show solidarity. From marching in protest to donating to organizations that fight injustice or build betters black communities, we can act.

In her blog, dockery cautions that we may say or do something that someone finds offensive, even if well intended. Making a mistake is okay but avoids the spiral of shame about saying the wrong thing. Instead, listen, learn, and then commit to doing better once we know what better is.

None of us can be good all the time. We still are part of a racist society with coded messages that black lives are inferior. Acknowledge this, and then lead the way towards real, systemic change through small and large acts of compassion.

We need to connect with those we work with. We need to acknowledge our differences and recognize when our biases interfere.

Inclusion goes beyond race, gender, and physical differences. It could be about how we interact with someone less experienced or in an entry-level role. Regardless of what or who, we should show and model human kindness. That's real leadership.

Chapter 8

Leadership Is Not about You

For about a decade, I've called Senior Master Sergeant Joel Rodriguez my friend. He calls me brother. Joel is different from most people I know. During our conversations, Joel always asked how he could assist me with something. When he offers, he means it.

Joel sincerely wants to help me achieve my goals. From helping me move my parent's furniture across town to giving me feedback, Joel has been there for me. He even gave me the first feedback about this book. Rarely does Joel ask anything of me, and I bet he's like this with family and just about everyone he knows.

Of all the colleagues I know, Joel has embraced and integrated the next leadership principle the best.

Regardless of riches, career level, or status, one resource that is equal among us is time. We each have the same 24 hours in a day, but we spend it differently. We value time so much that we'll exchange it for money. When we volunteer our time to help others, we're giving a great deal.

Joel volunteers his time, energy, and resources to help others. He'll place assisting others as a higher priority than what he might do otherwise, yet he expects nothing in return. Joel *Puts Others First*, which is the third leadership principle.

At the University of Illinois at Urbana-Champaign, I managed a team of students in a residence hall. A few weeks into the job, Sean, one of my students, dropped by my office with one of my friends to ask me about something. While we talked, I corrected Sean about something. I don't recall what it was, but about five minutes after they left, I remember how Sean returned alone. His face was red from fighting to control his anger. He told me not to criticize him in front of his friends.

Without pause, I told Sean he's right: I shouldn't have done that. I explained that this was my first time managing a team, and I just didn't think. By now, Sean's color returned to normal. I still remember his look of surprise as I made this admission. Before parting, I asked Sean, and later the team, to let me know when I make rookie mistakes so I can learn.

Acknowledging to Sean that I was wrong was a small act compared to other mistakes that managers make. Even so, this story illustrates another way to put others first: sacrificing ego.

Giving our time to put others first comes more natural for some, but recognizing and admitting our mistakes can be challenging for others. Leadership doesn't involve being defensive or building power. It is about apologizing when we're wrong and empowering others.

Sacrificing ego involves giving credit rather than taking it. When outcomes disappoint, it means accepting responsibility without blaming others or claiming that bad luck was involved.

Sinek writes about how sacrificing our time and ego helps inspire loyalty and a willingness for others to do the same.[31]

Putting others first can become contagious, especially when modeling critical behaviors that result in positive change. It is core to servant leadership.

Rather than believing that employees serve managers who serve the heads of business, servant leadership flips servitude. The CEO serves the executive board, ensuring they have the resources to achieve company goals. The executive board serves vice presidents who serve middle management. Managers serve employees who, in turn, serve customers. When companies change the servitude flow, great things happen.

In reflection, I think about all the people who have used their valuable time and energy to help me mature mentally and morally. Experiencing the amount of sacrifice for my benefit is humbling when not taken for granted. Because of how they contributed to my growth, I'm instilled with the desire to reciprocate and steward others.

Making our needs secondary by practicing stewardship is a way to give back to others. Still, it's also a rewarding experience that's full of enjoyment. Once started, it's hard to stop.

Chapter 9

You Won't Succeed through Command and Control

Have you ever worked for a department head who was into command and control? I have.

During an all-hands meeting, the Senior VP who I'll call Alan made an announcement. As of that meeting, Alan had ordered all employees not to speak to VPs. If anyone saw a VP walking in a hallway, we couldn't engage with them. If a VP called us, Alan wanted us to refer the VP to him.

Here's his rationale: employees—including managers and directors—could say something to an officer of the company who embellishes what was said.

Alan gave a recent example.[32] In an executive meeting, Ryan, the CIO, informed the other executives that Alan's department promised to complete a development project by the end of the quarter. Alan had no idea what Ryan was referring to and had not authorized any such project. When trying to explain that this wasn't true, Ryan interrupted and argued that Malissa, one of Alan's managers, made the promise.

It turns out that Ryan had talked with Malissa during a cross-functional project meeting. Ryan asked her if it was a good idea for her department to own the project. Malissa merely agreed that it was a good idea. Because Ryan exaggerated his conversation with Malissa, Alan outlawed VP engagement.

A couple of months after this ruling, I called a design meeting with some managers in Accounting. Before the meeting started and to my surprise, the CFO and four Accounting VPs walked in the room, and the CFO kicked off the meeting.

I was dumbfounded by this unexpected twist and didn't know what to do but proceed with the meeting. Afterward, I found my boss, explained what happened, and apologized for breaking Alan's rule.

Being the good guy that my boss was, he downplayed the event. A few hours later, though, I was called into the principal's office—I mean Ann's office, the department VP who reported to Alan. The experience wasn't pleasant, and my colleagues sympathized.

While this is an extreme example of command and control, I learned through my consulting that executives in other companies had a similar rule. In each instance, the effect was the same. With the combination of several controlling rules, the direct and indirect reports became frustrated. Some quit. Those who stayed suffered from stress, which affected their health. Productivity slowed down, and that triggered more rules.

Command and control erode relationships and hurt the health of the organization. Here's what one director told me: "If someone came to me and said that one person could devastate a department's culture, I wouldn't believe it. Having just gone through that experience and witnessed the negative spiral, I'm forced to believe that one person can cause that much harm!"

Giving Up Control is a critical leadership principle that complements the Put Others First Principle. Within leadership, power is intended to be shared. Those near the top of the hierarchy transfer power to those doing the work. Power transfer enables teams to achieve goals and help customers efficiently and effectively.

In contrast, those who hoard power limit the number of people who can leverage it, and then they use their power ineffectively.

Hoarding knowledge is hoarding power. At another organization where I worked, Doug, a technology manager, did this. Doug would compromise business managers like me by making us dependent on him. When he was sick or vacationing, we had a difficult time working with the technology department.

Like Doug, Dave Best had acquired a wealth of knowledge. For several years, he has worked for this company and has built a solid relationship with several EVPs and SVPs. He knew people.

Unlike Doug, Dave volunteered his expertise and insight to help his colleagues. He made working in the department easier and saved me a great deal of effort. By bestowing his knowledge, he became indispensable to his colleagues and me.

One more point: when the higher ranks share power, they share command and control. Doing so changes command and control to a shared responsibility and preventing employees from being dependent on a few to get things done.

Forcing employees to seek approval unnecessarily causes inefficiencies. At one company, I had to get a VP's authorization to pay a vendor $800. He was upset that he had to sign a request for something so trivial.

At another retail company, employees used an archaic point-of-sale system. When employees entered special orders, they had to find a supervisor for approval. With supervisors in meetings or working in other departments, sometimes customers waited twenty to thirty minutes to process the order.

Customers having to wait for supervisors isn't the point. When supervisors accessed the system, they didn't review the order. Instead, the only thing they did was click *approve*. Employees didn't make mistakes because of the built-in system checks. No one knew why approval was needed. The phrase, "That's the way we've always have done it," became, "Why do we do this to our customers?" The technology department eventually removed the approval requirement.

In *Turn the Ship Around*, David Marquet gives up control by turning followers into leaders and transforming the worst-performing nuclear submarine into the finest in the Navy.[33] When a few greedy people hold onto power, organizations become restrained, and progress slows down. Still, when we share power, our organizations become more energetic and healthier.

Chapter 10

Mistakes, Learning, and Growth

Of all the company executives who supervised me, none resembled Walter. As a VP of operations, Walter demonstrated how an officer of a company with an entrepreneurial spirit should perform to drive results. Although we worked in Operations, Walter leveraged his decades of sales experience to innovate how customers interacted with our company. He leveraged customer-experience theories before they became mainstream.

Walter wasn't perfect. I should note that I don't consider any of the professionals in my narratives to be angels or eagle scouts. Even the ones who I describe negatively aren't all bad. Including myself, we're a mix of good and bad stuff. Sometimes the bad stuff obscures what's good or vice versa. For Walter, I'll spotlight his good in one of the most memorable lessons that he taught me.

I was in Walter's office arguing about something that he wanted to be changed. To make this happen, I'd have to talk to several department heads about our new expectations about our partnerships. Departments would then have more work, which I didn't like and thought unnecessary. What's remarkable about this story isn't the change itself but how I delivered it.

Back in his office, I lost the argument. Walter dismissed me so I could begin informing the executives. I started with Accounts Management. Because I was a novice manager, you might guess what happened.

During my career, I've witnessed or heard about how others made the same mistake. When I talked with Andy, the Accounts Management VP, I explained what Walter wanted to do. I also discussed the additional tasks that we would require his account managers to do. Andy took the news better than I thought, and my fear of "shooting the messenger" didn't happen. Afterward, I continued to inform the department heads.

A couple of days later, I was in Walter's office talking about how the departments adapted to the news. When I finished my update, Walter asked a question.

"What did you say that made delivering the news so easy?" I can't recall what I said, but I doubt it was, "I told them this was your idea and not mine." I either answered dishonestly, or I omitted that I blamed Walter for the change.

In a serious but sympathetic tone, he explained to me the rules of engagement: In privacy, Walter expects his reports to debate and even object to how he wants to operate. As soon as we agreed upon a decision, Walter then expects us to implement it to the best of our abilities. When he makes an unpopular decision, Walter wants his reports to own it as if we made it.

He let me know that one department head asked him about his decision, exposing my attitude and dissension. Walter spoke about his disappointment with me and how poorly my approach reflected both on him and the company.

In the book, *The Advantage*,[34] Lencioni discusses the importance of commitment to final decisions and timeliness for its communication. While this applies to any team, I'll illustrate with a CEO's decision.

For any decision to succeed, one person needs to own and account for the decision. In this example, the CEO is the owner and has decided to restructure. Once made, the board needs to support, coordinate, and cascade the decision's message within the business units.

Openly disagreeing with a decision or not sharing the message at the same time hurts the board's reputation, reduces the opportunity to minimize complications, and affects the company's reputation. Consider what employees would think if their department were the last to know about restructuring. They probably wouldn't be too happy.

At all career levels, dissent happens when messengers want to avoid being blamed. It happens when they never buy into the message or didn't understand the reasoning behind it.

For the CEO example, executives who refuse to support the restructuring publicly model to employees an underlying dysfunction. At its worse, executives deliberately sabotage the restructuring plans with passive-aggressive resistance. These naysayers try to prove that the decision is wrong, resist helping, and when the initiative fails, blame the CEO. Within corporate America, we call this, *throwing someone under the bus*. A captain of a ship might call it a mutiny.

Messengers who dissent may not realize how they hurt themselves and the company, even when rebelling against a decision that won't work. People show more respect towards messengers who share the same, well-coordinated message than for messengers who openly disagree and blame the decider. If the plan fails and the team acts accountable and acknowledge that their decision was wrong, people can respect the group accountability. They may not like the results, but group accountability softens any harm caused by the decision.

Walter taught me a valuable lesson about what it means to be in management. I learned how crucial supporting company decisions are, regardless if I agree or not. While I didn't like to support unpopular decisions publicly, I knew that, privately, I could express to Walter how I felt.

The exception to Walter's rules of engagement happens either during or after implementation. If the team uncovers information that would have affected the decision, they're obligated to report revelations up the chain. New information could result in a reversal, additional contingencies, or acceptance but with no action.

My experience working for Walter changed me. Reflecting on my time with him, Walter supervised my work effectively. More importantly, though, I appreciate his mentoring and leading me to become a better manager.

Part of leadership involves mentoring and training others. Thinking about this, I'm reminded of a trendy quotation. It starts with one manager asking another, "What would we do if we trained our people, and they leave the company?" The second manager asks, "What would we do if we don't train them, and they stay?"

When leading, we think of others first and want them to become mentally and morally resolute. When employees are in a role too long, their development starts to plateau, and their work becomes less appealing. To continue leading them, we need to either find ways to keep developing them or help them move to a more challenging role.

With star performers, we benefit by having to spend less time developing them, which can be gratifying. What we may not understand is that keeping them may not be in their best interest and could be selfish. Instead, we should support their career development. Doing so may mean helping them find a more challenging role that continues to grow and develop them.

At one company, Rekia developed into a star performer. She worked for me for about a year. I encouraged her to apply for a role that she would find more challenging, for which the manager hired her. Before I left the company, Rekia received another promotion that had more significant responsibilities.

Managers who encourage employees to grow and leave improve their and the company's reputations. Former employees working in different organizations would speak highly of their previous team and company. If all managers did this, the broader workforce would perceive the organization as a preferred employer.

When I was a candidate for a Chief Learning Officer role, I talked to previous employees who are now in other companies. During one conversation, the employee said that she left the company to work for a prior manager in another state. If she ever moved back to Charlotte, she wanted another job in the same company because of how the managers supported employee growth and valued them.

In our teams, we want our teammates to achieve the extraordinary. We do this by encouraging them to develop mentally and morally. We accomplish this by modeling the right behaviors while coaching them to do the same.

One approach that managers have started to advocate is allowing employees to make mistakes. Terrence, the head of a large department, proudly announced that he wanted employees to risk making mistakes. He declared that management wouldn't use mistakes against them. That didn't happen.

When employees made mistakes that affected Terrence, he would remember. During performance reviews, the employee's manager would discuss the blunder and use it to justify a lower rating.

To interpret mistakes as learning opportunities, we need to change the department's environment. In this environment, managers empower and trust employees. Managers coach the less skilled while providing a figurative safety net. Doing so enables employees to build competence and confidence, and ultimately, enables them to contribute more substantially.

You don't have to be a manager to do this. As teammates, we can support each other with difficult work through coaching or mentoring (or both).

Leadership is about *Encouraging Change*, which is the fifth principle. Encouraging others to change not only helps them grow, doing so changes us as well. I've talked with mentors who explained to me that they learn as much or even more than the mentee, just by following the mentoring process.

Another way to encourage change is by enabling employees to find their solutions. When they come to us with a problem, challenge them to solve it. Have them describe the issue and ask probing questions to guide them. Ask how they would solve it, but don't give in and order a solution. Otherwise, we'll stifle their development and our ability to stimulate real change.

One day, I walked into Walter's office complaining about a technician who gave new meaning to being difficult. In the middle of fuming, Walter stopped me by saying, "This isn't my problem. Are you telling me about him because you want me to do something, or are you blowing off steam?" When I indicated the latter, he relaxed, smiled, and said, "Well, that's okay. Proceed to rant!"

When we believe that others have the potential to succeed but lack capability, coach them. If they are competent but lack confidence, then consult and encourage them. When they're competent and confident, step aside, and be amazed!

Chapter 11

The Blame-Shift

At one company, a VP asked me to be the acting manager of another team until she could hire a permanent replacement. Working with that team became one of my warmest memories about my tenure there.

I discovered that the team was not typical—they were rock stars who had developed a strong bond of support, awareness, and trust.

During the second team meeting, I asked how they wanted to handle an issue. What stood out for me wasn't the issue but how the team responded.

During the dialogue, one teammate would lead. The others would ask a couple of questions. Then another would lead while the rest asked questions. On they went. I was humbled at how quickly they innovated.

Some of what they generated wouldn't work. Still, as a team, they brainstormed and fine-tuned their solutions respectfully and powerfully.

The experience intrigued me because I didn't need to intervene. While they didn't exclude me, I didn't have to facilitate the conversation.

What I witnessed was blasts of rapid leadership in which the team took turns leading and asking exploratory questions.

When leading, the manager doesn't need to take charge or have all the answers. Neither does the manager need to be the smartest person in the room and have all the answers. Instead, the team shares in the leadership.

At one firm, I worked in the technology business unit. Due to a few corrupt partners, the firm had lost too many customers to stay in business.

When the firm closed the facilities and laid off about five hundred employees, someone shared with me how their HR department developed a unique process.

The employees knew that the job cuts were coming, and HR wanted to communicate who would be cut in as dignified way as possible. Instead of shepherding employees into a conference room, HR asked employees to call a phone number. They would hear recorded instructions for what to do if their job ended or how to proceed if they were still employed.

Because I learned this secondhand, I'm unsure if that's how their HR department did the layoff. Regardless, I told my boss what I heard.

The next day, he called me and said, "Gary, I shared what you told me about how that business unit handled their workforce reduction. Your idea of how we should do ours reached the CIO.

He's decided that's how our HR department will manage it."

I should note that the business units worked independently and in silos. So, the HR departments most likely didn't have a standard process or shared their approach with one another.

At the time, I was an individual contributor with no apparent influence. But leadership can come from anyone when we least expect it. Sometimes, the best ideas come from people in the field rather than executives at the top. That's what happened in my situation. I only knew the result because my superiors gave me credit as the idea worked its way to the CIO.

These stories illustrate two types of collaboration. The first tells how teammates collaborate by taking turns and rapidly changing from leading to clarifying. The second explains organizational collaboration, in which influence flowed from an unexpected source and involved several people sharing the information until it reached the CIO. *Collaborate with Others* is the sixth leadership principle.

For collaboration to work in teams, teammates need to interact as if leadership resides in each person rather than one, namely the manager. Because influence comes from all directions, teammates need to listen carefully to one another and ensure they understand the scope of someone's idea.

Collaboration also means that our focus is on whoever is leading and not ourselves. When conflicts occur or when people make mistakes, teammates work together to seek resolution. Holding themselves accountable, understanding the breadth of what's happening, and creating resolutions are the primary objectives.

Not all teams collaborate well. Project managers have told me about projects that failed. Too frequently, sponsors didn't want to hear about issues or warnings. If problems weren't at the sponsor level, the team members were more concerned about themselves. They neglected to think about the overall project.

Project teams that fail to reach their goals tend to avoid collaborations and have faulty communications. Both cause misunderstandings and errors. When things go wrong, individuals quickly shift to protecting themselves by finding someone to blame for failures.

Failing to collaborate happens at the organizational level as well. When executives optimize their departments, they can hurt how other departments perform. Much of the time, this is inadvertent, and departments don't realize how their changes affect different groups.

Through research and his consulting, Rummler concluded that organizations share the same anatomy and identified six fundamental organizational laws.[35] Relevant to department improvements is Rummler's third law. It states that when one component of an organization's system optimizes, the organization often sub-optimizes.

When VPs improve how their departments operate, they tend to manage the improvements in terms of their organizational chart. If initiatives are to strengthen the organization, VPs need to focus on enhancing the primary business process. After identifying process improvements, only then should VPs discuss implications for how departments should divide process responsibility.

When VPs focus on department improvements without involving other VPs, silos form. As different departments are affected by changes caused by another department, they react from the perspective of their silo, and the system sub-optimizes. Over time, VPs become territorial, and the CEO can't understand why performance drops.

As a board, senior officers need to think systemically and focus on what's best for strengthening their processes. While doing this enables organizations to achieve their enterprise goals, few boards know how.

When teams and departments start collaborating and focusing on achieving enterprise goals, blaming others and avoiding accountability diminish. I call this the blame-shift in which teams shift from blame to resolving problems. When the blame-shift transpires, teams and departments communicate more effectively, expose issues, become accountable, and fix them. When this happens, egos aren't threatened, and organizations perform strongly.

Chapter 12

Knowing about Leadership Is Not Enough

"I have the heart of a servant leader!" Those were the words of Stephanie, a VP at a Fortune 500 company. Stephanie was addressing her department at an all-hands meeting. What Stephanie said wasn't close to the truth.

Stephanie mastered leadership sound bites and recited them when lecturing the company's employees and speaking publicly. I admit, she fooled others who didn't work for her, and Stephanie skillfully convinced audiences. She even won over a well-known consultant and colleague of mine who adores who he perceives her to be.

If we questioned Stephanie about leadership, we'd begin to see hints of command and control in her logic. If we observed her actions and decisions, we'd see through her façade. Like a tower built of cards, if we moved one card, the deck would collapse.

I had the impression that Stephanie wasn't trying to fake practicing leadership but believed she effectively led her department. Maybe Stephanie didn't recognize how her leadership knowledge wasn't congruent with her behaviors.

If you read this book, my previous one, and all the books about leadership, the knowledge you'd gain wouldn't be enough. That would be like having medical residents read books about open heart surgery and expecting them to be proficient. If doctors operate on me, their capabilities better rely on more than book-knowledge!

Attending leadership workshops, reading books, and watching videos can build our knowledge. The next step is to practice what we learned. Disappointedly, knowledge with practice still isn't enough to develop leadership.

The third step is feedback. As humans, we have programmed biases and blind spots. As Ronald Graves, my leadership coach, told me, "You can't see the whole box if we're in it. We need someone outside the box to share observations and provide the right feedback at the right time."

Feedback serves two purposes. First, it enables us to know that our performance is off and what we should do to improve it. Second, it confirms that our performance is what we need it to be. When we learn from a coach that our behaviors will produce the desired results, we build confidence.

You can leverage multiple ways to gather feedback. One way is to let the people we work with know that we're studying leadership and want their help as we practice what we've learned.

Here's how to get people you work with to help. Ask them to observe your behaviors. Encourage them to go as far as writing changes that they see in you, both positive and negative. If they don't find any difference, ask them to tell you. Later, ask how well you're doing.

Another approach is through 360-degree feedback. With this approach, someone other than you surveys colleagues, bosses, direct reports, and customers to collect insights into your leadership practices.

A note of caution: you need a skilled evaluator to assess the results. During a video podcast, Don Tosti warns that 360-degree feedback yields multiple opportunities that can be overwhelming.[36] Qualified experts present feedback in a way that won't overwhelm. They interpret what the feedback means and help you identify the one behavior to improve. After improvement, experts can help with the next behavior.

After identifying the behavior to improve, let others know. If you discovered that an old habit had affected someone, apologize, and explain how you're trying to change. Later, ask others how you well are developing.

Another is Marshall Goldsmith's Feedforward technique.[37] Here's how it works: start with a behavior that you want to change. For example, you might want to communicate more effectively through email. Find someone you know and describe the behavior that you want to change. Ask the person for two ideas on how you can become better. The person can only share ideas about future changes. If the person knows you, she can't talk about your past behaviors and what you did wrong. While she shares, your only task is to listen intently and comprehend. Take notes. Commenting or even agreeing with them is out of bounds. Don't even say, "That's a great idea!" Instead, don't talk. When your colleague finishes, your only response will be, "Thank you." That's it.

When you finish, you can offer to reciprocate. Have the person think of a behavior she wants to change, and then follow the steps.

By the way, coaching works. I have a coach who has helped me greatly. Instead of taking my word that coaching works, Joseph Grenny shares a coaching story that might explain how coaching can lead to better outcomes.[38]

Phillip and Ray are two rookie tennis players with identical tennis skills. For a day, Phillip plays tennis with a skilled opponent while a coach observes. At crucial moments, the coach stops the play, corrects Phillip's form, and allows them to proceed. During breaks, the coach discusses tactics, and Phillip practices them later. By the end of the day, Phillip has not only received feedback, but he also practices the feedback repeatedly until the coach confirms that Phillip is performing effectively.

The same day, Ray plays tennis with a comparable opponent but without coaching. By the end of the day, I'd wager that Phillip's tennis skills are better than Ray's.

To lead effectively, we need to *Develop Our Leadership Practice Continuously*, which is the seventh leadership principle. We develop leadership by learning about leadership, practicing what we learned, and then gather feedback. After that, we repeat the process. You might call this *Learn > Do > Assess*. After the assessment, we improve our practice using the feedback. We assess some more, fine-tune our behavior, and repeat. Regardless of age, experience, or career level, we can always learn. With a growth mindset, that's how we roll.

If we're strong at learning and receiving feedback, we'll strengthen our leadership practices enormously, so let's do it!

Chapter 13

The Problem with Traditional Leadership

For one of my first jobs, I became a senior instructional designer working in a talent development department. I was assigned to work with Victor, a managing director, to develop a training program for technology risk consultants.

I flew to Dallas to meet Victor's team and plan the project. For the first meeting, Victor couldn't attend due to travel. I started to get to know his team, though and began planning the program.

When I finally met Victor, I felt intimidated and out of place. I had a hard time believing that Victor would listen to me because I was only an individual contributor.

At this company, I found managing directors to be smart, insightful, and creative. Victor was no exception. I was impressed with his ability to explain technology risks and marketplace challenges. I spent a great deal of time listening and learning.

As we started developing the program, I realized that Victor and his team looked to me for guidance. I didn't notice this at first, probably because I was distracted by not being in a position of authority and by my intimidation. Later, I learned that they wanted to work with a training expert. As I began to guide and help them achieve their goals, I gained their respect. This experience taught me that even though I may not have the title, I can still influence.

Twenty years later, I've influenced hundreds of executives and managers without the need for formal authority. If we ignore titles, treat everyone with respect, and assume that the people we work with have the best intentions, great things happen. That's how I learned to work with others.

As you may have experienced, not everyone has a positive approach. People who predominately view life through a fixed mindset misunderstand the meaning of leadership. They tend to fall prey to traditional thinking about authority and how to work with others.

Traditional leadership is about collecting and controlling followers. They proclaim themselves leaders and behave in ways that I'm about to describe.

Think of leadership as a way of practicing a role. It involves a collection of actions that are independent of titles or positions of authority.

When I use the term *leader*, I'm referring to those who believe in traditional leadership. Unless I'm referring to a traditionalist, I seldom use the term. Too many have associated *leader* with a position of power or a synonym for an executive or manager.

Leadership is about action rather than being. While a semantic challenge, I associate *leadership* more as a verb than a noun.

I've met executives who call themselves leaders but fail to lead. I've worked with teammates who were without a position of power but led better than most senior managers and executives. I've learned a great deal from these people and are drawn to connect with them.

Leaders, at their worst, gather followers to serve them. They may proclaim that they are servant leaders. Still, their actions demonstrate that they serve themselves at the expense of others. Without care or remorse, they'll use blameless employees as scapegoats and fire them to save their reputation and control. I've seen this happen and had this happen to me.

This story surprised me: an HR director shared how a VP told her to restructure his organization so he could get rid of a director whom he didn't like. When executives can't legally fire someone, they eliminate the employee's position, which is easier to rationalize and defend.

Speaking of easy, that's a primary motivator for leaders: they want to do things the easy way with quick fixes to resolve short-term problems. If employees threaten a leader's authority, get rid of them. "Forget long-term consequences," thinks the leader. "I'll deal with those problems later."

To recognize someone who's a traditional leader, here are some signs to watch out for. Look for people who want to be the hero and save the team. I call this as *heroship*. If a manager acts like he's the smartest person in the room, we may have a leader. If someone argues that getting close or friendly with subordinates shows weakness, we may have a leader. If people hoard power and believe that giving away power weakens them, watch out!

Finally, if executives treat employees as less valued than operational costs and willingly lay off employees while retaining their salaries, we've uncovered traditional leaders. How many times have we heard about CEOs receiving bonuses for maintaining profits by reducing labor? If companies have frequent layoffs during downturned economies, they're using the easy solution instead of working on creative ways to cut costs without the expense of human capital.

Fortunately, these are extreme examples, and not everyone becomes trapped thinking this way.

When we begin working in the corporate world, we may think traditionally. With experience, we learn that using influence is more effective than relying on authority.

When I worked at a Fortune 500 company, I presented a plan to Kimani, the head of the department. The project was to change how we managed our documentation. Kimani was okay with my proposal and asked me to communicate it to the department. "I can't do that," I objective. "Because you're in charge, I thought you'd announce it."

Typical of Kimani, she waved an imaginary wand and proclaimed, "I waved the wand of power and grant you empowerment. Figure out how you'll communicate your plan and then just do it. You'll be fine, but I'm here if you need me."

Kimani made her point, and I was fine. People listened, and the department adopted the solution.

As we gain experience and learn about leadership, either through formal training or watching others model effective leadership, we begin to discard traditional assumptions. We build momentum, change cultures for the better, and nurture others. Then, we help build leadership with those we influence.

Chapter 14

Epilogue: *What* and *Why* Do not Get You to *How*

After the publication of *Nine Practices*, I started talking to audiences about what leadership is and why it's important. After speaking to members of the Union County Chamber of Commerce in North Carolina, one attendee raised her hand. She said, "All this leadership stuff is great, but none of what you said talks about how I can lead. So how do I learn to lead?" The member was right: I didn't explain how to lead.

The *what* and *why* doesn't get us to *how* it's done. In a way, *What the Heck* is like many other leadership books that define the term, share stories to model behaviors, and imply how it's done. I do that in *What the Heck* and explain underlying principles that guide leadership practices.

If you want to understand *how*, you can read *Nine Practices*, which includes *how* to lead and *how to learn* leadership. In it, I share nine practices that you can apply to different types of situations. If you want to learn more about these practices, download a PDF from my website. It's titled, *Description of each of the nine practices*.[39]

If this becomes the first of a trilogy, the second book, *How the Heck Do I Lead?* would explain the *how*, while the third book, *How the Heck do I Train Others to Lead?* would explain *how to learn* leadership. Alas, authors often plan manuscripts but without beginning them. However, I'll do what I can to complete the next two books soon!

I've been thinking about the content in *What the Heck* for about five years, and I'm glad to have put pen to paper. I hope you found what I produced to be insightful and valuable. If not, let me know so I can learn. I would be honored for you would lead me.

Chapter 15

Dedication Postscript

Why I, as a black man, attend KKK rallies is the title of Daryl Davis' powerful TEDxNaperville video.⁴⁰ A few years ago, I watched this video, and still today, I'm moved by Daryl's eloquent words, curiosity, and courage.

Possibly because of my inexperience, I struggle to find the words to articulate my feelings about the unjust divisiveness and harm towards Americans just because of their appearance. Daryl, however, has organized his thoughts and expressed himself in a humbling way. The French say, *le mot juste*, which means using the right words at the right time. For me, Daryl's words are timeless.

Daryl Davis' talk begins with his relationship with Robert White and how they became "the best of friends." What's difficult to conceive is how different these friends are.

Davis is a professional musician, while White worked for the police department. When they met, White had just finished serving a second prison sentence for assault with the intent to murder two black men. Earlier, White served time for conspiring to bomb a Baltimore synagogue. White was the Grand Dragon of the Ku Klux Klan in Maryland.

Near the beginning of his talk, Davis describes his first experience with racism and shares his reaction:

> "It was inconceivable to me that someone who had never laid eyes on me, never spoke to me, knew absolutely nothing about me would want to inflict pain upon me for no other reason than this: the color of my skin...I don't know why people felt that way, but I realized that there are some people who did...How can you hate me when you don't even know me?"

Davis grew up exploring why this hatred happens. He shares one profound explanation and rare insight:

> "Ignorance breeds fear. We fear those things we do not understand. If we do not keep that fear in check, that fear, in turn, will bread hatred...If we do not keep that hatred in check, that hatred, in turn, will breed destruction. We want to destroy those things that we hate. Why? Because they cause us to be afraid but guess what? They may have been harmless, and we were just ignorant."

As of today, a certain online book store (starts with an "A") lists

Robin DiAngelo's book, *White Fragility*,[41] as the third bestselling book. It was number one, but the books by Mary L. Trump and John Bolton sit at number one and two.

In a Seattle Channel video,[42] DiAngelo adds some clarity to why racial hatred occurs:

> "...if we don't know our history, if we cannot trace the past into the present, we cannot explain current conditions in ways that are transformative rather than victim-blaming...these struggles are never separated from the present. At the same time, a piece of white fragility is that white people are not taught their history."

After hearing this, I realized that my history classes had a fundamental gap that failed to explain the American experience. What I learned in my all-white school was the white American, male, heterosexual, Christian history.

It wasn't until this month that I learned about Black Wall Street and its history. I'm frustrated with my ignorance of American history and the secondary educational biases that limited my historical knowledge. Now that I'm aware of this gap, I'm trying to correct the omission.

I write this postscript, not because of this omission, but because Daryl Davis offers a unique way of influencing to create substantial change. For Davis, respect is the key, and the following quotation describes his technique.

What resulted from using his technique, along with his showing respect, is this: White left the KKK. He gave Davis his KKK robe and police uniform. Davis describes his technique this way:

> "Take the time to sit down and talk with your adversaries. You will learn something, and they will learn something from you. When two enemies are talking, they're not fighting. They're talking. It's when the talking ceases that the ground becomes fertile for violence. So, keep the conversation going."

Davis notes that he's a musician and not a psychologist or sociologist. He states, "If I can do that, anybody in here can do that."

If you find his process to be uncomfortable like I do, then do what you can. From small acts of kindness to protesting or serving in government, we can make a difference. Doing so can help reduce and mitigate the factors that trigger the murder of unarmed black Americans.

As we learn to act, maybe we can risk stepping beyond our comfort zone and aspire to Davis' approach. We can begin to construct the elements needed to develop a bond with those who are different from us—maybe even resulting in *the best of friends*. If so, we can realize what many consider impossible: the maturation of real inclusiveness and celebration of diversity without fear or feeling threatened. This could be a path that builds character. This is leadership.

Acknowledgments

For about five years, *What the Heck* was in my head, but I never seriously considered dipping the pen into the ink. This year, though, I made a decision that changed everything. I had no idea the effect that would have on my professional career. The decision wasn't to write this book.

In late January, Ronald Graves started coaching me. Ronald is a Certified Business Leadership Coach. He is the Founder and President of the Poiema Leadership Institute and is on the John Maxwell Team. Ronald lives his life with a lifelong learning attitude. He's also a kind friend and colleague.

Through his coaching, Ronald nudged and guided me as I reexamined habits that have held me back. That process triggered an unexpected inspirational moment: I realized that I needed to write this book, and so I did. Thank you, Ronald.

Colleagues and friends have helped me along the way, which I acknowledged in *Nine Practices*. On that list, I'd like to add Peter Popovich, Felix Nater, and Lisa Toenniges. They've checked in on me from time to time just to find out how I'm doing and to offer encouragement. So often, people in our lives have no knowledge of the effect they have on others, but too often, we don't find and thank them. Thank you, Peter, Felix, and Lisa.

Finally, I'd like to thank Denise Chapman, Peter Popovich (again), and Jim Schultz for sharing with me some technical mistakes that I made in an earlier draft. Their feedback has helped me improve the quality of the final product.

About the author

I'm that guy who stops his car, gets out, and moves a turtle to the side of the road. When I'm not rescuing turtles, I'm serving cats. When I'm not serving cats, I'm helping people lead more effectively. When I'm not assisting people to lead, I'm working with organizations to strengthen their leadership-development programs.

Before writing leadership books, I've worked at universities as an administrator and spent sixteen years working in corporate America. Since then, I've moved on to writing and consulting.

Throughout my career, I've managed large and small teams. I've made plenty of mistakes and missed opportunities. Still, I've matured from these experiences—at least, I hope I have.

Even though I've accomplished much, I'm still learning. I continue to search for ways to push myself outside of my comfort zone.

One of my best career decisions was joining ISPI[43]. At their conferences, I met scholars and practitioners who shared their craft with me on a personal level. I consider some, like Guy W. Wallace, to be good friends. Being a part of an association is a great way to grow professionally because of the many members who sincerely want to help one another.

You can learn more about me and my other books through my website, https://www.garyadepaul.com.

What the Heck Is Leadership and Why Should I Care?

Unlike leadership books that focus on competencies, Gary DePaul explains nine practices that anyone—regardless or role—can use immediately!

Recipient of the ISPI 2016 Outstanding Performance Communication Award, Gary DePaul explains how leadership is radically changing.

"Gary has saved anyone with an interest in the topic of leadership a tremendous amount of legwork and created an incredible resource for leadership growth. Most importantly, the rich assortment of examples, practices, and recommended actions provided are a tremendous asset to our development and growth as leaders. A note of caution: be prepared to see yourself and your own leadership assumptions and practices challenged (in a good way)."

Rick Rummler, President of The Rummler Group
Co-author of *White Space Revisited: Creating Value through Process*

"Gary DePaul's comprehensive *Nine Practices of 21st Century Leadership* makes sense of the vast sea of leadership books. Written with both managers and scholars in mind, DePaul's study situates—and demystifies—the language of leadership in systems thinking. In 15 well-organized and lucidly written chapters, the author builds a series of metaphors to explain the practices of expert managers—analyzing, detecting, guiding, nurturing and more. This book will change your thinking about leadership."

Edwin Battistella, PhD
Author of *Sorry about That: The Language of Public Apology*

"If you believe that the broad aim of clinical instruction is about teaching medical procedures, you're wrong. Whether an attending, a faculty member, or another type of clinical instructor, believing this can hinder the learning process."

Granted, a large part of clinical training involves instructing medical procedures. But this isn't enough for preparing professionals for practicing as specialists or subspecialists.

"I read this book with great interest as someone who works with the healthcare profession to adopt the evidence-based principles and practices of human performance technology. Gary does a great job integrating sound learning theory and performance improvement insights that focuses on producing valued results the patient and caregiver want. I highly recommend this book to any healthcare professional who wants to climb to a higher achievement level of impactful learning events and performance outcomes."

Tim Brock, PhD Director of Consulting Services of the ROI Institute, Inc. Faculty, United Nations System Staff College (UNSSC)
Author of "Simulation Operations, Curriculum Integration, and Performance Improvement in *Healthcare Simulation: A Guide for Operations Specialists*

Implicit Association Tests (IAT)

Project Implicit® is a nonprofit that educates the public about hidden biases and to collect data using the Internet, their 'virtual laboratory.'[44]

The organization's national and international researchers collaborate to study implicit social cognition, which means the thoughts and feelings outside of conscious awareness and control.

Project Implicit offers two groups of tests:

Project Implicit Social Attitudes Tests
Discover your implicit associations about race, gender, sexual orientation, and other topics:
https://implicit.harvard.edu/implicit/takeatest.html

Project Implicit Health
Discover your implicit associations about exercise, anxiety, alcohol, eating, marijuana, and similar subjects:
https://implicit.harvard.edu/implicit/user/pih/pih/index.jsp

Endnotes

Below are the referenced endnotes. One distributor wouldn't list my book unless I removed links to a competitor. To access the links, you'll need to download the bibliography PDF:

https://www.garyadepaul.com/WhatTheHeck

[1] On the following pages is a list of names and ages of those who lost their lives to law enforcement. The primary source is from Rich Juzwiak and Aleksander Chan, *Unarmed People of Color Killed by Police*, 1999-2014, https://gawker.com/unarmed-people-of-color-killed-by-police-1999-2014-1666672349 (accessed June 4, 2020).

[2] If you're disappointed that I don't include a bibliography, I've tried to accommodate you by creating a list of leadership and related books, which you can find on my author website. Give this a try: https://www.garyadepaul.com/WhatTheHeck.

[3] Joseph Grenny is the lead author of *Influencer: The New Science of Leading Change*. The others are Kerry Patterson, David Maxfield, Ron McMillan, and Al Switzler (you can find the link in the bibliography PDF). Grenny is the cochairman and cofounder of VitalSmarts.

[4] Simon Sinek, *How Great Leaders Inspire Action*, TED,

https://www.ted.com/talks/simon_sinek_how_great_leaders_inspire_action (accessed June 4, 2020).

⁵ Simon Sinek, *Start with Why: How Great Leaders Inspire Everyone to Take Action*, (you can find the link in the bibliography PDF).

⁶ Simon Sinek, *Leaders Eat Last: Why Some Teams Pull Together and Others Don't* (you can find the link in the bibliography PDF).

⁷ Liz Wiseman with Greg McKeown, *Multipliers, Revised and Updated: How the Best Leaders Make Everyone Smarter* (you can find the link in the bibliography PDF).

⁸ Peter also shared with me some websites where you can learn more about EQ. These are worth reviewing. Travis Bradberry and Jean Greaves are the authors of *Emotional Intelligence 2.0*, which includes an EQ assessment and 66 strategies, https://www.talentsmart.com/products/emotional-intelligence-2.0 (accessed June 29, 2020). The Six Seconds EQ Network is a nonprofit that offers resources, events, and certifications, https://www.6seconds.org (accessed June 29, 2020). Daniel Goleman, author of *What Makes a Leader: Why Emotional Intelligence Matters*, offers several resources and services, https://golemanei.com (accessed June 29, 2020).

⁹ Simon Sinek, *#SimonSays, Management vs. Leadership*, https://www.youtube.com/watch?v=sr0d_HbbbcQ (accessed June 4, 2020).

¹⁰ Roger Addison & Carol Haig, *Performance Architecture: Where Geary Rummler's Work and Business Process Intersect*, https://www.bptrends.com/performance-architecture-where-geary-rummlers-work-and-business-process-intersect (accessed June 4, 2020).

[11] Ideas on Management, *Mary Parker Follett (1868–1933)*, http://ideasonmanagement.blogspot.com/p/mary-parker-follett-1868-1933.html (accessed April 23, 2020).

[12] I also discuss this in Chapter 10, "Mistakes, Learning, and Growth."

[13] L. David Marquet, *Shout Out to Southern Gas Association*, https://www.youtube.com/watch?v=sSSx8FjVWss (accessed June 12, 2020).

[14] L. David Marquet, Captain, US Navy (Retired). *Turn the Ship Around! A True Story Turning Followers into Leaders* (you can find the link in the bibliography PDF).

[15] Gary A. DePaul, PhD., *Nine Practices of 21st Century Leadership: A Guide for Inspiring Creativity, Innovation, and Engagement* (abbreviated: *Nine Practices*) (you can find the link in the bibliography PDF).

[16] Carol S. Dweck, *Mindset: The New Psychology of Success* (you can find the link in the bibliography PDF). Carol Dweck, *The Power of Believing that You Can Improve*, TED, https://www.ted.com/talks/carol_dweck_the_power_of_believing_that_you_can_improve (accessed June 2, 2020).

[17] Believing that Michael Jordan is a gifted athlete implies that his basketball talent is a natural ability. This belief implies that some are born with certain talents. I reference Jordan later.

[18] In contrast to believing that Jordan is gifted, this belief recognizes his hard work and dedication to improving his athletic capabilities. He may have been born with physical characteristics needed to excel at basketball, but this belief assumes that physical characteristics aren't sufficient to become a great basketball player; you need consistent practice with the right feedback as well.

[19] This story is near the beginning of her Mindset book.

[20] Kevin and Jackie Freiberg, *Nuts! Southwest Airlines' Crazy Recipe for Business and Personal Success* (you can find the link in the bibliography PDF).

[21] Harvard Business Review Staff, *How Companies Can Profit from a "Growth Mindset"*, https://hbr.org/2014/11/how-companies-can-profit-from-a-growth-mindset (accessed June 3, 2020).

[22] Hilary Scarlett, *Neuroscience for Organizational Change* (you can find the link in the bibliography PDF).

[23] August Public Inc., *Amy C. Edmondson Talk on Psychological Safety* https://www.youtube.com/watch?v=m00QU4UnphQ (accessed June 6, 2020), and Amy C. Edmondson, *How to Turn a Group of Strangers into a Team*, https://www.ted.com/talks/amy_edmondson_how_to_turn_a_group_of_strangers_into_a_team (accessed June 6, 2020).

[24] Since writing this chapter, I learned more about the origins of the psychological safety concept. The easiest definition that I found is the following: "Psychological safety is about removing fear from human interaction and replacing it with respect and permission." cited in Wikipedia, *Psychological Safety* https://en.wikipedia.org/wiki/Psychological_safety (accessed July 8, 2020). The referenced citation in Wikipedia is from one of the best articles, written as a Q/A with Timothy R Clark, is from InfoQ, *Author Q&A: The 4 Stages of Psychological Safety* https://www.infoq.com/articles/book-stages-psychological-safety (accessed July 8, 2020).

[25] Patrick M. Lencioni's describes this as Vulnerability-based Trust (VBT) in *The Advantage: Why Organizational Health Trumps Everything Else In Business* (you can find the link in the bibliography PDF).

[26] Kevin and Jackie Freiberg, *Nuts! Southwest Airlines' Crazy Recipe for Business and Personal Success* (you can find the link in the bibliography PDF).

[27] Here are some example letters that CEOs made public: *CEO Satya Nadella to Microsoft employees, Change in Ourselves Helps Drive Change in the World*, https://blogs.microsoft.com/blog/2020/06/05/change-in-ourselves-helps-drive-change-in-the-world; *CNBC, Read Nike CEO John Donahoe's note to employees on racism: We must 'get our own house in order'* (letter embedded), https://www.cnbc.com/2020/06/05/nike-ceo-note-to-workers-on-racism-must-get-our-own-house-in-order.html; Memphis Business Journal, *First Horizon CEO addresses protests, societal injustice in letter to employees*, https://www.bizjournals.com/memphis/news/2020/06/04/first-horizon-ceo-bryan-jordan-addresses-protests.html (all accessed June 8, 2020).

[28] ESPN, *Panthers cut ties with CPI Security after CEO's comments on police brutality*, https://www.espn.com/nfl/story/_/id/29276795/panthers-cut-ties-cpi-security-ceo-comments-police-brutality (accessed June 8, 2020).

[29] Sporting News, *Michael Jordan: $100M pledge is a way to 'make a stand' for African-Americans who've been 'beaten down'*, https://www.sportingnews.com/us/nba/news/jordan-brand-michael-jordan-donate-100-million-racial-equality/nauuavp48vbt17mv3sfatr7go (accessed June 8, 2020).

[30] Tiffany dockery, *Please Stop 'Just Checking In' on Your Black Co-Workers*, https://zora.medium.com/please-stop-just-checking-in-on-

[31] Simon Sinek, *Leaders Eat Last: Why Some Teams Pull Together and Others Don't* (you can find the link in the bibliography PDF).

[32] I don't recall the details about this example, so I've guessed at some of what happened. The explanation, though, was similar to this example.

[33] L. David Marquet, Captain, US Navy (Retired). *Turn the Ship Around! A True Story Turning Followers into Leaders* (you can find the link in the bibliography PDF).

[34] Patrick M. Lencioni, *The Advantage: Why Organizational Health Trumps Everything Else In Business* (you can find the link in the bibliography PDF).

[35] Geary Rummler, *Serious Performance Consulting According to Rummler* (you can find the link in the bibliography PDF).

[36] Guy W. Wallace, *Don Tosti—HPT Practitioner 2008*, Tosti discusses feedback around 06:15, https://www.youtube.com/watch?v=hG53a2QXx5s&feature=youtu.be (accessed June 10, 2020).

[37] Marshall Goldsmith, *Try Feedforward Instead of Feedback*, http://www.marshallgoldsmith.com/articles/try-feedforward-instead-feedback (accessed June 10, 2020).

[38] Joseph Grenny, Kerry Patterson, David Maxfield, Ron McMillan, and Al Switzler. *Influencer: The New Science of Leading Change* (you can find the link in the bibliography PDF).

[39] Gary DePaul, *Nine Practices* webpage, https://www.garyadepaul.com/Nine-Practices-of-21st-Century-Leadership (accessed June 5, 2020).

[40] TEDx Talks, *Why I, as a black man, attend KKK rallies | Daryl Davis | TEDxNaperville*. https://www.youtube.com/watch?v=ORp3q1Oaezw (accessed June 27, 2020).

[41] Robin DiAngelo, *White Fragility: Why It's So Hard for White People to Talk About Racism* (you can find the link in the bibliography PDF).

[42] Seattle Channel, *Dr. Robin DiAngelo discusses 'White Fragility'*, https://www.youtube.com/watch?v=45ey4jgoxeU (accessed June 27, 2020).

[43] International Society for Performance Improvement, ISPI, https://www.ispi.org (accessed June 27, 2020).

[44] Project Implicit, About Us, https://implicit.harvard.edu/implicit/aboutus.html (accessed July 7, 2020).

www.ingramcontent.com/pod-product-compliance
Lightning Source LLC
Chambersburg PA
CBHW070234220526
45465CB00004B/1421